ARCTIC Diary

Surviving on thin ice

SAM AND RICHARD BRANSON

First published in Great Britain in 2007 by
Virgin Books Ltd
Thames Wharf Studios
Rainville Road
London
W6 9HA

A catalogue record for this book is available from the British Library.

ISBN 978 0 7535 1356 9

The paper used in this book is a natural, recyclable product made from wood grown in sustainable forests. The manufacturing process conforms to the regulations of the country of origin.

Typeset by Phoenix Photosetting, Chatham, Kent

Printed and bound in Great Britain by CPI Bookmarque Ltd, Croydon, CR0 4TD

Contents

Acknowledgements

Thanks to Will Steger and the Will Steger Foundation; thanks to Nicole Rom, Executive Director, and Jerry Stenger; thanks to John Stetson, Ed Viesturs, Abby Fenton and Elizabeth Andre for generous use of their trail journals and despatches that helped fill in the dots.

Thanks to the Inuit people we met along our journey for being so welcoming, kind and generous with their knowledge. And thanks to mother nature for providing such a fascinating and an ever awe-inspiring world for us to live in.

A short note from an old dog

I am very proud of my son Sam who, although born into privilege, is a regular person, sensitive and caring towards other people, and passionate about certain issues. So when Will Steger, of the Steger Foundation, invited us to go on an expedition to the Arctic, one of the harshest and most dangerous places in the world, to check out the effects of global warming, I could think of no one I'd rather go with than Sam.

I have always believed that people should never accept anything at face value, but should always check things out for themselves – and I hope I have passed that message and sense of purpose on to my children. I couldn't have asked for a better son and daughter. Sam's sister Holly, for example, has chosen to become a doctor and heal people – especially vulnerable children. Sam, who is younger, is still feeling his way to some extent, but he has a great sense of being at one with nature and an all-encompassing sense of spirit and place. Like me, he is dedicated to making sure that we do no harm, and one of the best ways to do this is to be educated about what *does* harm, to us and our amazing world.

Because I have such a deep love for the natural world and the last remaining wild places, with all their incredible diversity, for many years I have done all I can to protect them.

For example, I don't believe that industry and businesses have to be destructive to the environment. We can work, earn a living and be responsible at the same time. I am doing all I can to ensure that Virgin is a responsible, non-polluting group. Our people have a brief, which is to look at every possible way to maintain or improve the state of the environment. We switch off, waste nothing, recycle – on top of which I am investing billions in developing new, green biofuels for our transport businesses.

I might beat the drum a bit – but if we mess up this world, we can't just take off to a nicer, cleaner, safer one. We have no choice – we're stuck with this world and it with us. We have to make sure that we don't screw it up.

I'm happy to say that Sam has shared in this concern since he was a child. We have often talked about the environment, especially when on our island home in the Caribbean, or in Africa, wonderfully natural and organic places where the air really is clean. But for how much longer will it stay clean? Sam has been part of the discussions when, as a family, we have debated how we could ensure we did no harm, whilst at the same time enjoying ourselves, having fun and living normal lives, unfettered by any sense of being obsessive about it. Native peoples who live simple, traditional lives do no harm to our planet, yet you would never call them cranks; so why are people who really care often seen as slightly nuts?

I've always been very hands-on and I have a sense of great curiosity about everything – how does it work, why does it work, what makes it tick? If I don't understand something, I'll find someone who does – there's always someone who knows more than you do. But you don't have to have lots of degrees to be an expert, though two of the people I have learned a great deal from do have an impressive array of qualifications. Tim Flannery – who wrote one of my 'bibles', *The Weather Makers* – is an explorer, conservationist, paleontologist, field zoologist, geologist, academic and the writer of over a dozen books. It's been said of him that he has discovered more new species of animal than Charles Darwin.

And few environmental scientists can match James Lovelock for achievement. He's a chemist, physicist, inventor and planetary diagnostician who taught NASA a few things. He was honoured in 1997 with the Blue Planet Prize, which is widely considered the environmental equivalent of a Nobel Prize. One of his many books, *Gaia* in 1979, set me on the road to appreciating that the environment was not indestructible. James Lovelock believes that Gaia – or 'Mother Earth' – is a single living entity which maintains the conditions necessary for her survival. She can heal herself when threatened – but even with something unfathomable and fabulous as Gaia, there comes a tipping point beyond which nothing will help. I've called my particular brand of environmentally responsible business 'Gaia Capitalism' in honour of James Lovelock.

In his book, *The Lives of a Cell*, Lewis Thomas, a medical doctor and author, describes our world as a single living organism beautifully:

> Viewed from the distance of the moon, the astonishing thing about the earth, catching the breath, is that it is alive. The photographs show the dry, pounded surface of the moon in the foreground, dry as an old bone. Aloft, floating free beneath the moist, gleaming, membrane of bright blue sky, is the rising earth, the only exuberant thing in this part of the cosmos. If you could look long enough, you would see the swirling of the great drifts of white cloud, covering and uncovering the half-hidden masses of land. If you had been looking for a very long, geologic time, you could have seen the continents themselves in motion, drifting apart on their crustal plates, held afloat by the fire beneath. It has the organized, self-contained look of a live creature, full of information, marvellously skilled in handling the sun.

Like Lewis Thomas and Tim Flannery, James Lovelock believes that we are perilously close to reaching the tipping point, when the world will not be able to 'handle the sun'. When Will Steger asked me to go on his Global Warming 101 Expedition to check out what was happening on the 'Front Line' – the Arctic – it didn't take much to persuade me, other than timing. Could I take several months off at the start of 2007 to go on a long expedition?

I talked it over with Sam and we both immediately agreed that we wanted to go to see for ourselves the condition of one of the world's most fragile and vulnerable places. Some of the most knowledgeable people about the environment - people without a single degree between them - are men and women of the wild, people who understand the seasons, the animals and the patterns of life. Their knowledge has been handed down, not just for centuries, but through generations for thousands of years. You only have to talk to an African elder, or someone who has always lived in the Amazon, or the Australian outback to know this.

I knew that the Arctic is more susceptible to the damage of global warming than anywhere else. What happens to the rest of the world in terms of climate change often happens in the Arctic first, the shift in animal migrations and populations. But I had never talked to the people of the Arctic Circle - the Inuit. This was the ideal opportunity to do exactly that.

By going to the Arctic together, Sam and I would have the chance to share the lessons I first learned when I was young. It would also be an opportunity for us to spend some time together in a good cause. As you can read in my autobiography *Losing My Virginity*, and the extended version of *Screw It, Let's Do It*, I am passionate about the environment and Gaia Capitalism. I wanted to see what else I could learn that I could apply to Virgin's environmentally friendly way of working - and Sam was also very enthusiastic about expanding his mind and spending time with an almost mythical people who are struggling to survive in an ever more fragile place.

By the time I came to leave him to continue onwards without me, I learned that my son was a man, something that had almost slipped by me unnoticed, as it does with many parents. He gained the respect of the people he was with - all of them experienced Arctic expeditioners - and has been invited back. Next year, he will be going with them on an extensive expedition to Ellesmere Island in the high Arctic to make more observations.

Sam wrote a diary while he was away. I read it on his return and was so touched I thought it would make a great book - so I invited KT Forster, the folks at Virgin Books and Rosemary Kingsland to work with us on turning his diary into a message that other people of his age would enjoy and relate to. His generation is very important because they are the ones who face the challenge of ensuring that Gaia survives. They are the ones who must clean up the mess that began with the Industrial Revolution. This world is the only home we have. It gives us everything – our life, food and shelter. In the same way we protect our families and all we cherish, we must do all that is in our power to protect our world and help ensure that all the people on it have safe and viable environments. I hope you will enjoy going on our journey with us and will want to learn more.

Now, over to Sam . . .

Richard Branson

In the beginning ...

In the spring of 2007 Will Steger, a renowned arctic explorer, asked my dad and me if we would like to join his Global Warming 101 Expedition to the Arctic to highlight climate change. The idea was to travel across Baffin Island – which is mostly within the Arctic Circle – talking to the Inuit people, the natives of that region, to ask them what they had observed about climate change and how it was affecting their lives. Being there on the ground the Inuit, more than anyone, would be able to tell us – and the world – what was going on.

The Arctic had been in the news a lot and few people had not seen pictures of floes melting and hungry polar bears swimming across miles of empty sea before eventually drowning. Walruses were starving because the fish they feed on have gone to cooler depths. In some areas, ice was so thin and unstable that thousands of grey seals hauled themselves out onto barren rocky islands to give birth. Unable to make secure insulated dens in the snow, safe from polar bear predators, they watched helplessly as storms and high tides washed some fifteen hundred newborn seal pups out to sea.

Birds and fish never seen so far north before – and even hornets – were arriving. Reports were coming in that told of significant changes in the region's ecosystems. Storms were brewing up over warmer seas; coastal villages were lashed by rainstorms instead of snow. Species that had adapted over 40,000 years to one kind of weather were having to adapt to another. Some will make it, and some probably won't.

The expedition's mission was to discover if this was really happening, and, if so, on what scale.

It seemed to Will Steger that Baffin Island was a microcosm of the Arctic, and by talking to real people about their everyday lives, we would come back with a strong message to pass on to the world. Could everyone unite into one people with a common aim – to stop or slow down global warming? It seemed a worthwhile challenge.

Dad went because not only does he understand what global warming is doing to the planet, he is doing something about it by investing all his profits from his transportation businesses (i.e. the airlines) into alternative green fuels and technologies. He has also initiated a $25 million prize – the 'Virgin Earth Challenge' – to inspire innovations to combat climate change. I wanted to go because I am from the next generation – and it is my generation that is going to have to live with climate change in the future. It will be up to us to sort it out if nothing is done soon. We should be getting involved, or at least educating ourselves about it so we can do the right things to help even in the smallest ways.

I am in a fortunate position to experience these things first-hand and I want to share with people what I have seen. I am young and still a real novice and don't totally understand the issues myself, but I am learning slowly just like everyone else. I want to make sure that people don't think I am preaching to them – just giving them an insight to my experiences and my feelings, so they can make their own judgements.

How do you put an expedition to the Arctic into words? It is a place travelled by few, and most of those who have been there call it home. Most of the others who go are tourists there to marvel at the strange unearthly beauty of the landscape and the animals that live there, from polar bears to whales. A few go with a sense of sadness mixed with wonder, for they know now that the Arctic is fragile and the ice and snow might soon vanish. Its frozen grip is loosening; there is a historic reshaping of the icy world. Even the dark arctic night is getting lighter, thanks to a warmer layer of air reflecting light from the sun over the horizon.

Weathermen said the weather patterns were getting 'very strange' – while Inuit elders, who had always been able to predict the weather, found they could no longer do so. Would hunters run into a blizzard? Would fishermen in their kayaks be overturned by rougher seas? It was becoming impossible to tell. If you look back in history, there have been warming periods, as well as cold periods. Each time, the situation reverted to normal. This time, nobody seems to know what will happen.

Despite this, Will Steger thought the Inuit would have an idea of what the long-term changes might be. While we in our cosy Western homes have become disconnected from the natural world surrounding us, the Inuit are connected to their environment and wildlife. They sew parkas from sealskin. They mush to work. And even now they use all the elements of nature around them for living. Traditional Inuit life is a model of carbon neutrality, yet the Inuit are the first witnesses of climate change, heralded by rising tides and receding ice.

They are the early warning, the world's sentries. They see what's happening to the planet, and give the message to the rest of the world. The environment they live in is so extreme it has become a sort of visual measuring board for our planet's rise in temperature. We wanted to see what warnings they were giving us that we needed to heed.

Some of the messages were very close to home for Dad and me. We spend a large part of the year in our idyllic Caribbean home, a small island named Necker. I have been there every summer since I was born, and learned to swim and sail and surf. But changes in the Arctic are already affecting the far-off tropics. Warmer seas are killing coral reefs in the Caribbean. During my 22 years there I have noticed some great changes.

Scientists have found that 30 per cent of the world's CO_2 emissions are absorbed by tropical rainforests – yet huge tracts are being slashed and burned every day. Melting polar ice would lead to rising sea levels worldwide. The pessimistic projection is that if both Arctic and Antarctic ice sheets melt at the current rate, sea levels will rise by some fifty feet by the year 2100. Low-lying islands and coastal communities will become extinct. Millions of people will be forced from their homes, becoming refugees, and even maps will have to be redrawn.

I hope this will not happen. People might be careless but, just as there comes a tipping point beyond which almost nothing will stop extreme climate change, there is a point when even the most careless person realises that something has to be done. But it's only by messengers carrying the news about obvious and visible signs of global warming that people far away from the front line will realise what's going on.

The Arctic is the front line.

When we went on the Global Warming 101 Expedition, it was to act as observers and messengers. Along the way I experienced things that will stay with me for the rest of my life. I hope that in some way, as my experiences are put onto paper, it will give you the opportunity to lend your own presence to this wondrous place and give you a better insight into a part of our world that is not only mysterious in its beauty, but a marker board for our rapidly changing climate.

I think the world is like one big umbrella. We all live under the same umbrella – but what if the rain comes from underneath?

Many people might say, 'It's not my problem. So what if a few icebergs are melting? It's happening too far away to affect me.' But nature has no borders or boundaries. I think people have become so concerned with borders and their own countries they have forgotten we all live in the same place without imaginary lines. It's one world. I think global warming will bring people together from different parts of the world to act as one body for the same cause. It will help people to realise we are all as vulnerable as each other to the elements of nature.

One depressing fact is that the very people who go to see these lovely, wild and inaccessible places might be doing even more harm. We all know that dark things absorb more light and heat than light things (white clothing in summer, dark clothing in winter) – and soot is no different. Soot, or black carbon, absorbs sunlight, so soot-covered ice reflects less light as well. It's changing the way sunlight reflects off snow and ice.

According to NASA scientists, soot in areas with ice and snow may play an important role in climate change. Black soot may be responsible for 25 per cent of observed global warming over the past century. When soot-covered snow and ice begins melting, the warming effect increases – the layers of soot become more concentrated on the snow's surface.

As glaciers and ice sheets melt, they get even dirtier. You can actually see it when you stand and look up at a melting glacier – there's a thick layer of brownish grime. When polar ice caps start to melt, less sunlight gets reflected back into space. Temperatures start to rise as more sunlight is absorbed into the oceans and land, and this causes even further melting.

And where does a lot of this soot come from? From diesel engines. Diesel is used in the Arctic regions because it has a lower flash point than petrol. Diesel-powered tour buses and some of the older snowmobiles are some of the biggest spewers of soot and pollutants. Snowmobiles are very heavy and can fall through thinning ice. More and more Inuit are turning back to dogs and sledding after almost half a century of snowmobile travel. This is why we used dogsleds on the expedition – to show that the carbon-neutral traditional ways of the Inuit are best and that dogsleds can reach the most inaccessible places.

In the same way, white ice and snow are reflective, throwing back the sun's rays; but as the snow stops falling and the ice melts, dark rocks and the ocean are exposed. They absorb heat. The more heat the sea absorbs, the warmer it gets. The warmer it gets, the faster the old ice cover melts.

One of the places the expedition went to on Baffin Island was Pangnirtung, a little coastal village on a dramatic sea fjord, surrounded by soaring mountains. The usual snow that had been there for a thousand years was missing and it was dangerous to walk on the wind-blown glare ice and frozen rocks. The Inuit hunters there knew what was happening. 'The world is slowly disintegrating,' they said. 'They call it climate change. But we just call it breaking up.'

Before you begin reading the diary, I thought I should mention that I have kept it in pretty much the same form as when I wrote it, at the end of each day, tired and cold in my tent. If some of it doesn't make chronological sense or seems slightly bitty, then it was probably written on a night when I was rushing to get to sleep! I hope you enjoy reading it and take from it what you can.

Here's tons of stuff about the expedition

I thought it would be useful if I let you read what the Will Steger Foundation sent to inform us about the expedition and its aims. There's a map as well in the photo section, so you can follow the dotted line to see the route. I think it's important to say that the team had been on the trail for about three months before my dad and I arrived to join them. My experience was intense - so imagine how much more so theirs was. They took great deep gulps of global warming and observed and heard about many more examples of the way in which the oceans are warming than I did. But what I experienced was enough for me to want to know a lot more and to help to do my bit. If you want to know more about Baffin Island - and some of the other things I mention in my diary - I've dipped into the old books (and in some cases, I do mean old) and written up a few pieces that you can find at the back under 'The Heavy Stuff' - not too heavy, I hope. I've tried to make it easy to dip into. It's wicked how you can get hooked on history, once you start rooting about.

Educators and explorers Will Steger, John Stetson, Elizabeth Andre and Abby Fenton will join three Inuit hunters on a 1,200-mile, four-month-long dogsled expedition across the Canadian Arctic's Baffin Island. The expedition will be travelling with Inuit dog teams over traditional hunting paths, up frozen rivers, through steep-sided fjords, over glaciers and ice caps, and across the sea ice to reach some of the most remote Inuit villages of the world. During the weeklong visits to each Inuit village, the team will listen to and document the Inuit experience with climate change. These collected images, sounds and stories will illustrate the dramatic climate-related changes happening in the Arctic: starving polar bears, retreating pack ice, melting glaciers, disrupted hunting and travelling, and the unravelling of a traditional way of life.

The Inuit Voice

Because of its remoteness, the great changes in the Arctic regions go unseen in our media. The Inuit people, the polar bears, and all life in the Arctic have no voice. They are the innocent victims of global warming; the stories they tell of their daily lives will show that it is real. The expedition will be recorded through a documentary film that will help educate people around the world about the plight of the Inuit people and put a human face on a problem that will soon consume us all.

The Expedition Route

The expedition will depart from Iqaluit, Baffin Island, the capital of Nunavut [Nunavut is the Inuit land on the northeast side of Canada], for a 1,200-mile journey starting during the second week of February 2007. Following the frozen McKeand River over the Hall Peninsula, the expedition will cross Cumberland Sound to the community of Pangnirtung. The expedition will spend at least one week in each of the five communities along the way to document the native people's observations of the rapidly changing climate. The emphasis will be on interviewing the elders — to hear their stories of the past and their concerns for the future. These elders, many of whom are in their eighties, remember the days before the influence of Western culture on their society, and they provide an important historical perspective to our changing times and climate. It will be important to document the stories of their era before it vanishes.

The varied topography of the route offers some of the best Arctic photographic and documentary opportunities of North America. Dog teams and other hunters from villages along the way will be joining the expedition en route. Once across the mountains, the expedition will travel on the sea ice along the Atlantic side of Baffin Island.

There they will visit Qikiqtarjuaq (formerly known as Broughton Island) and Clyde River, two of the most remote communities in North America. These villages rely on the sea ice to obtain their food, and the dramatic shortening of the winter season is having a profound effect on their way of life. Leaving Clyde River, the expedition travels west to cross the rugged mountains of Baffin Island.

Along the route the team will travel along the southern edge of the Barnes Ice Cap, a remnant of the past Ice Age. Upon reaching the east coast of Baffin the expedition will cross the pack ice of the Foxe Basin to their destination at the community of Iglulik, the cultural centre and ancestral home for the hunters and dogs of the Canadian Inuit. Their people settled in Iglulik 2,000 years ago and, until recently, the currents that flow from the Hudson Bay to Lancaster Sound have provided ample hunting. The cold, fifty-below winter freezes the moving water solid for eight months of the year, but global warming has disrupted these weather patterns and, by extension, the entire Inuit way of life. The traditional

Inuit calendar is based around the hunting seasons e.g. spring is the seal-hunting season. The recent warming has reduced their hunting season by 50 per cent, and the people say that, if these were traditional times, there would be great starvation.

The Expedition Crew

They were a wonderful team, totally dependable and great fun to be around. All were knowledgeable, friendly and more than willing to do their share two hundred per cent. It was an unimaginable feeling to be around Inuit hunters, and to learn the lore of the land from them. Could we live in that harsh and astonishingly beautiful environment? I knew I would find it pretty tough. (See page 177 for more details of the crew and their experiences.)

Will Steger – Team Leader. Runs the Will Steger Foundation, a non-profit educational organisation, based in Minnesota.

John Stetson – Expedition Manager. Sled dog trainer. Runs dogmusher.com.

Abby Fenton – Education Co-ordinator and expedition member.

Elizabeth Andre – Education Co-ordinator and expedition member.

Nancy Moundalexis – Dog trainer and expedition member.

Theo Ikummaq – Expedition member and Inuit partner. Hunter and explorer, lives in Iglulik, Nunavut.

Lukie Airut – Inuit hunter, celebrated carver and Canadian ranger. Lives in Iglulik, Nunavut.

Simon Qamanirq – Inuit polar bear hunting guide, carver, Canadian Ranger. Lives in Iglulik, Nunavut.

John Huston – Expedition Base Camp Manager. Wilderness and Arctic expeditioner and writer.

Jim Paulson – Webmaster and Expedition Technology Logistics.

Jerry Stenger – Expedition cameraman and Producer.

Ed Viesturs – America's foremost high-altitude mountaineer, one of the most successful Himalayan climbers in American history. Lives in Washington State.

Sarah McNair-Landry – Arctic explorer, kite-skier, Grew up in Iqaluit.

And finally ... three more members of the team. I didn't do my write-up. If I had, I'm not sure what I would have said. Maybe just a single phrase: 'Warning – carries L plates'.

Otto Brockway
Otto was born on the 7 November 1984. At 22, he is an experienced and very talented film maker. He started making music at a young age and then moved on to making music videos. He made many videos for emerging urban artists and had his films shown on Channel U and MTV Base. He has now put his focus into documentary making and recently returned from Peru, where he is planning to film the lost tribe of the Ashaninka.

Sam Branson
Sam was born in England on 12 August 1985. At 21 this makes him one of the youngest members of the team. He grew up in between England and the Caribbean and has a great respect for nature and all the elements within it. After school he

trained as a chef at Le Cordon Bleu and then went on to do a year's diploma in music. Since he was young he has always had a love for extreme sports, ranging from racing motocross to surfing. He jumped at the chance to join the expedition and it looks like he's going to embrace everything this environment throws at him.

Richard Branson

What can I say? How about John Huston's description: 'If Richard Branson had been born an animal he would have been a lion — a fun-loving lion. He's a prankster and a joker and a lot of fun to be with.'

That's my dad!

Sam's Diary

Or

My journey to the Arctic starts here

Wednesday 18 April 2007

We spent last night in Ottawa, at the Westin Hotel. Otto – who happens to be my cousin – is here on the expedition as a cameraman. Otto and I both chilled out when we arrived. I was trying to suck in all the cushty things in the hotel. I remember savouring my bath, thinking, 'I know there's going to be a time soon where I would give anything to soak my body in hot water.'

We went out to the Hard Rock for a burger and a beer and chatted about what lay ahead. I haven't skied since I was eleven and was getting a bit nervous about the short period I had in which to learn again. And in what conditions. I have never been to the Arctic before. Most of our adventures and sporting activities have taken place in warm, even very hot, places, like the Caribbean or Africa. The Arctic is a great unknown.

Thursday 19 April

This morning Otto and I met up with Daryl. He's one of the producers of the documentary that will be made of our trip. A really nice guy. Grabbing our bags, we jumped on the plane and headed off to Iqaluit, which is way down south on Baffin Island. Iqaluit means 'place of many fish'. It is also the capital of Nunavut, which is the huge Inuit territory around the Hudson Bay area of northeastern Canada. On the way over we chatted about the whole project and Otto started filming. We're shooting on high-definition Sony V1 cameras. Initially chatting in front of the camera was quite strange but I'm slowly getting used to it. Looking down you could see huge ice slabs drifting in the sea. It was quite a sight. The further into the Arctic we travelled, the more solid the ice became.

With a slight shiver of anticipation, I realised that these were real bergs! From our height, it was hard to gain a perspective that would give me an idea of their size. I thought of the Titanic hitting an iceberg, of walruses, seals and whales. It really was another world. I was in the middle of reading a fantasy book – *Northern Lights* by Philip Pullman – about magic in the high Arctic. Those icebergs below were no fantasy – but it was magical.

Iqaluit has the longest runway in Inuit territory – it's long enough for international planes, so the town revolves around the airport. Once we landed, the icy air hit us with a shock, like jumping into a bath filled with ice cubes. It caught at my throat, froze my nostrils and made my eyes sting. A few days ago, I was in London during the hottest spring on record. People were moaning about having no air conditioning and saying things like, 'If this is spring, what the hell is summer going to be like?' I'm used to the heat, so didn't mind temperatures in the mid-30s. Now here I was, plunged sharply into minus 10 centigrade. Otto had come from filming in South America, so it wasn't less of a shock for him either. But as we walked to the buildings, it seemed to get warmer out of the wind. It wasn't too bad after all. We grinned at each other, hunched into our down parkas, and met up with Sarah McNair-Landry. This is almost her home town. Her parents – both famous explorers – moved here when Sarah was three and used the town as their jumping-off point for the Arctic. She's just finished the first leg of our expedition and is now heading off to race the team from the BBC's *Top Gear* programme – the UK's most popular motoring show – up to the North Pole. I was chatting to Jeremy Clarkson, *Top Gear*'s larger-than-life presenter, who is here to film a show. They are trying to race a team of dogsleds, led by Sarah, to the North Pole in a Toyota pick up. Richard Hammond, another presenter of the show, will be on Sarah's team.

Sarah crossed the Arctic by dogsled last year. The year before she crossed the South Pole unsupported. Soon she is leaving on an unsupported kiting expedition south-north across Greenland. Will Steger wanted us to meet because I think (if I can prove myself here) he wants us to join him on a six-man team across Ellesmere Island next year, to see the collapsing ice shelves. Sarah will be on that expedition with her brother, Eric. They've both been around this part of the world for a long time, and understand it in all its moods and nuances. I have skied before, but most of my experiences have been in more balmy parts of the world, where I learned to surf and sail. I hope that I can keep up and prove that I'm up to this unique challenge.

Iqaluit itself is flat, treeless, sprawling, with mostly functional buildings. It was originally named Frobisher by the navigator and explorer Martin Frobisher, who discovered it about five hundred years ago. He had found the back door to China. He just couldn't find a way through the ice. Iqaluit expanded fast in the 1940s when the US built a big air base here because they were convinced that the Russians were about to send a few missiles over the North Pole. The DEW (Distant Early Warning) line was established – the stuff of the Cold War and spy thrillers. But all that has gone. Now, Iqaluit seems like the old Wild West, but without the action. It's a quiet town with a real sense of family community. The population here is 7,000. It's quite endearing to see the mothers walking around with their kids on their backs peeking out with rosy faces and huge dark eyes. Their clothing is a big thick jacket with a huge hood, and the children are carried in the hood – just like a kangaroo's pouch.

After meeting Sarah we found our flight up to Clyde River had been cancelled due to bad weather. I'm now sitting in our room. We're staying in one of the local college dorms. It's great to see snow everywhere and I'm slowly getting a better picture of what awaits.

Tonight Daryl, Otto and I met up with the *National Geographic* guys and Ed Viesturs for dinner. Ed is a really friendly, laid-back guy. He is widely regarded as America's foremost high-altitude mountaineer. He has reached the summits of the world's fourteen 8,000-metre peaks, including Everest and K2, without supplemental oxygen. He is joining us on our crossing of the Barnes Ice Cap. About wanting to come on this trip, he said, 'I jumped at the opportunity to go to the Arctic with someone as experienced as Will Steger. After many years of leading and guiding my own expeditions, I'm looking forward to being an apprentice and learning all I can about dog-sledding, Inuit culture, climate change and the Arctic environment.'

The *National Geographic* guys are interesting; one of them is a veteran presenter, Boyd Matson (who does some pretty tough assignments for National Geographic Explorer Channel) and the other a cameraman who works at the base in Washington – Jason Ofranon. After a drink and some food Otto, Jason and I decided to walk out over the frozen sea ice next to the town. It was beautiful to see the stark, barren terrain all around like a painted landscape on the moon. Strange to think we were standing on sea not land.

The ice was about eight to ten feet thick, and somewhere beneath us, fishes swam. The light on the ground was unearthly. That sunset tranquil colour – soft greens, gold, mauves, orange, gradually fading to a pewter shade and then ghostly silver. It lasts for hours, though, as the sun sets very slowly.

What really shocked me was the cold as the sun slowly went. It doesn't give much heat – but even a couple of degrees makes a difference. A chill wind got up, blowing in from the frozen sea and vast ice fields of the North Pole. I got goose bumps. Taking off my gloves to take pictures was a real shock. It's the sort of cold that chills to the bone. When we first landed I thought to myself that it wasn't going to be as cold as I first imagined. I realised I was wrong. It's going to be a lot colder!

Friday 20 April

What a day. This morning we left Iqaluit on a twin-engine Otter and headed for Clyde River, over the sea ice. It was breathtaking. Jagged, snow-covered mountains were visible for miles against the bluest of skies – it was like a panoramic photograph, all blue and white. The massive bulk of the Barnes Ice Cap was like icing on a large cake, glittering in the morning sun. Diamonds seemed to flash off it, and crevasses made dark striations like the scratching of an ink pen. It was a mysterious world that I had heard so much about, and I was in awe at the thought that soon I would be there.

As we came in to land you could see the ice edge where it meets the sea, some distance from where the shoreline probably was, judging by the position of a few markers and some docks. A few icebergs were stuck in the frozen ice, like ice cubes in a giant's drink. We seemed to be aiming straight for a narrow fjord with vertical walls a thousand feet high, before turning again to make another run in from the sea. From the air, the airstrip looked almost non-existent – like a flat strip of ice, like all the other flat strips. My mind drifted to hidden rocks and crevasses and plane wings touching and flipping us into a somersault. Perhaps you get what you wish for! The landing was a little sketchy. We had to circle the runway a bit while waiting for them to clear it.

When we landed it felt like we were going to slide off the runway. I think we hit some ice, but everything was fine. It's strange, I never used to be a nervous flyer but I go through periods of it. A couple of weeks ago, I was with my dad and Ted (my granddad) in a balloon soaring above majestic Mount Kenya. Far below, we could see the little thatch huts of the Masai, and elephants plodding slowly along. Dad loves balloons – as I do. But I'm not sure that I could have done what he has done, ripping along at 200 miles an hour in a jet stream 40,000 feet above the Pacific, or climbing out of a balloon capsule that was taller than Nelson's column, to sit on the top gazing down at the Atlas Mountains as they rushed up to meet him. And who else but my dad would walk a plank between two balloons? Compared with any of that, landing on a little snowy beach in the Arctic in a bouncing plane is child's play.

Clyde River is known as Kangiqtugaapik or 'nice little inlet' to the Inuit. Located on a gravel flood plain, in the shelter of Patricia Bay, on the eastern shore of Baffin Island, the town is surrounded by spectacular fjords that stretch all the way to the Barnes Ice Cap. The mountains, icebergs and glaciers in the Clyde River area attract rock and ice climbers from around the world. The area is also home to a wide range of animals including caribou, ring seals, narwhal, polar bears and a variety of other wildlife. The Iqalirtuuq National Wildlife Area, a protected bowhead whale sanctuary, is located in Patricia Bay. The 100-ton bowhead was a summer visitor, so it would be a few more weeks before they came, but blue whales and sperm whales also cruised by. I am familiar with the biggest land animals on the planet, but would I be lucky enough to see the biggest marine animals?

Of the approximately 800 residents in Clyde River, about half are under the age of 18. The town is home to a post office, fire station, church, two grocery stores, a community library and family resource centre. Though people lived and travelled throughout Home Bay and the northeast coast of Baffin Island for generations, where they once lived in igloos, Clyde River did not become a permanent settlement until the arrival of the Hudson Bay Company in 1923. The company relocated many Inuit families to the area to support the growing fur industry. Much of the trade was for Arctic fox pelts, later shifting to seal skins, highly prized in Europe at that time. Throughout the 1960s almost all of the remaining Inuit families were moved off the surrounding land into permanent settlements and Clyde River grew considerably in size. During World War Two a US Coast Guard weather station was established in the village, providing an alternative source of income as the fur trade declined. People today work in a variety of jobs, including teaching, municipal works, law enforcement and wildlife management. Many people continue to live a traditional life tied closely to the land.

We were met by the team and taken back to the team house. We're all staying in one of the Inuit's homes. His family is in one room and the other Inuit hunter is in another room and we're all sleeping on the floor on our camping mattresses – though Otto has a different room. It's pretty cosy but it's good having everyone together. It's a perfect way to get to know the team.

It all seems really organised. Will Steger has been working nonstop and seems quite quiet and very focused. You can tell he has a big vision and is working full speed to get it fulfilled. The rest of the team are all friendly and obviously live with no pretence. They are all very capable and most of them have grown up in a wilderness of some sort.

I have always found it easy to relate to people who have a love of nature. A lot like I find with surfers. I have often dormed like this. The last time was in Fiji where I went to catch some good waves. My friends and I slept on a flea-infested mattress in a storage room as there were no other rooms available. We woke up every morning covered in bites. It was an amazing place called Sigatoga, right by the river mouth. The surfer community is a very free and friendly one and people will crash out anywhere, cramming into a room with travellers who haven't washed for two weeks – some snoring, farting, belching . . . great when you're trying to sleep, but it's a good laugh. Sharing stories of the biggest, scariest waves and the most fun we've ever had surfing. I look forward to sharing some of that camaraderie on this trip, learning of new things, different experiences.

After we settled in I was issued with my gear. It all looks very hard-core and is covered in sponsorship logos. It's really cool to have gear with my name on. Automatically I felt like part of the team and I realised that I was part of something really special.

After lunch we went to watch an igloo-making contest. Our two Inuit hunters ended up in first and second place. It was fascinating to watch how they built them, sawing into the snow and cutting out blocks, then spiralling them up. It's a real skill. What I didn't realise is that half the space is created by the cuts into the floor. You go below ground level to get into it. Once your body heat melts the inside of the igloo it freezes and forms the strength of the structure. One of the hunters and guides who will be going with us, Theo, actually had his wedding in an igloo that fit 150 people. (If you want to know more about igloos there's more at the back under 'The Heavy Stuff'.)

The village of Clyde River is much smaller than Iqaluit. People are very friendly and the language is very different. It is spoken words, but the way they pronounce things reminds me of the way some tribes in Africa communicate. It is a sort of clicking sound. A lot of people speak basic English, but it's hard to understand the accent. The main language here is Inuktitut.

After the igloo building Ed Viesturs and I went off with John Stetson for some training with the dogs. We pulled his sled out to where the dogs are kept on the sea ice, tied in a long line. My first reaction was one of surprise. There must have been about a hundred dogs out on the ice and hearing them all howling was frightening. It was like coming face to face with a pack of wolves and your instinct is to run and climb a tree. Only there's no tree. You're out there with them on a flat white billiard table, a quarter of a mile from the village, and there's nowhere to hide. They were tied, but the line was just kept in place with a couple of pegs hammered into the ice. I eyed them very warily as we approached. Their barking and leaping against the line grew more agitated and at any moment I expected this tidal wave of ravening wolf-dogs to overwhelm us. With one shout from John they were all quiet. Man, I was really surprised at the size of some of them. They must be waist high, about the size of a Great Dane or an Irish Wolfhound. They are absolutely beautiful but within a split second can turn into the most terrifying-looking creature ever. All of the aggressiveness is aimed at the other dogs, though, and I soon realised that if you are confident with them and show that you are dominant they are fine to handle. John showed how to put the harnesses on the dogs and how to set it all up.

It's amazing to see how excited they become when they see us getting ready to drive. They are born to run and they love it. Later, I learned that the twenty expedition dogs are Stetson's own dogs – they are descendants of the dogs that Will Steger used to breed during the 1980s and 90s for his epic expeditions across the Arctic and Antarctic. The dogs are a cross between a Siberian husky and an Alaskan Eskimo dog, so they are quite a bit larger than your average husky or malamute. The Inuit Eskimo dogs are smaller and with a far thicker coat. This makes a difference when running during hotter days. It was amusing to see that Stetson's dogs wore little jackets when the nights got really cold. I realised then that he really loved his dogs – and they him. It was a symbiotic relationship, based on love, trust and a lot of respect.

The terrain was impressive and the dogs seemed to move at a steady pace. John obviously knows his dogs well and told us some of the commands. It's interesting to see the differences between the way the Inuit drive their dogs and how others do. The Inuit sit on their sled and direct the dogs by a forty-foot whip, whereas the others use vocal commands. The Inuit crack the whip out one side and the dogs turn the other way.

In the snow where the dogs are kept there were cut-up seals, some frozen upright in the snow. The Inuits feed the meat to their dogs.

The temperature out here varies from about -11°C in the day and -25° at night. It's the wind-chill that gets you, though. Even on a sunny day a slight breeze can be tough to handle. It's when you realise your hood is your saviour. The fur used is generally wolverine, and very justifiably used. It's a revelation how much wind it blocks out. My little (but not that little) friend has been like an ice cube in my pants for the last day!

After a rest and an early dinner John Huston (Base Camp Manager), who's a very capable young guy, kitted us out with some cross-country skis. John went on the 'Race to the Poles' trip. I remember watching him in a documentary before I came out here.

The skis are very thin and not very easy to get used to! Ed, John and I headed out over the frozen sea to the old village about a mile away. It's abandoned now. It took a while to pick up a rhythm. Trying to ski in mukluks – the soft Inuit boot – is difficult. They're a bit like Ugg boots with soft material up to the knee. There's no support for your ankle and the different terrain (ice and snow packs) makes it even harder. After quite a few falls I started to get used to it. The wind really picked up while we were out there but moving around keeps you surprisingly warm. Mukluks are important in sub-zero temperatures. When Victorian sailors and missionaries first came, they insisted on wearing their regular clothes, even down to bowler hats and ordinary leather boots. In their journals they recorded how the Eskimos (as they called them) tried to get them to wear their furs and skins – but they refused and soon got frostbite.

I've just made my bed and we're now chilling out watching some of Mickey's (the film director) other work. It's been a nonstop day and I know I'm going to sleep like a baby.

Saturday 21 April

This morning I woke up and we had our daily 9 a.m. meeting. We discussed the schedule for the day and logistics of filming. Simon, one of the Inuit hunters, announced that one of their friends had died. Three hunters went out hunting and one of them died en route. They haven't worked out why. This meant that the whole town was in mourning and the village activities (including the 1 p.m. dog race) were cancelled. As the village is small there is an overwhelming sense of community. When someone dies, everything shuts down and the community pools together some money to help the family in their time of loss.

After the meeting John took Ed and me (with Otto filming) out on a dog drive. I found putting the harnesses on the dogs a lot easier this time, but when they get excited they start to fight so once they're hooked up you have to be quick. The calls for the dogs are as follows:

    Left — Ha!
    Right — Geet!
    Stop — Woow!
    Move on — Onby!
    Forward — Hike!

We went out for about two hours and the weather was great. I found travelling by dog team could be a bit unpredictable, because no matter how well trained the dogs are, they are always temperamental. You never know if they will listen to you or if they'll leave you dragging behind. After we got back we had to unharness the dogs and tie them back up. To do this I had to take my outer mitts off and my hands absolutely froze. The pain instantly bit deep, as if my hands were clamped in a frozen vice. As the ache spread, I could feel my bones, as fragile as brittle dry branches in an ice forest. I felt that if I banged or knocked them, they would splinter and chunks would fall off. I held them and blew, trying to get some warmth back. No one can prepare you by telling you how fierce real cold can be – you have to experience it. You have to be so careful. Expose yourself to the wind at big cost. If it's windy you can get frostbite in thirty seconds. After lunch I had a ten-minute chat with Dad on the phone and a twenty-minute power nap. There is so much to take in that I feel mentally and physically exhausted. But I don't want to miss anything.

About an hour after lunch John Huston took Ed and me for another ski. John always carries a pump-action shotgun with him just in case we come across any polar bears. It's loaded with a firecracker-type cartridge to scare the bear, and if it doesn't work he carries real shots as a last resort. I think that's when it came to me just how potentially dangerous it is and how vulnerable we were out here. At game reserves in Africa the game wardens also carry rifles, but somehow, I never think of them having to use them. Images of charging polar bears filled my mind. White on white – it would be hard to see them against the snow until you were practically on top of them. I'd been told that usually they loped off when they heard people – unless they were very hungry. How do you tell if a bear is hungry?

We headed north out the back of town and followed the hills. I've got the hang of it a little more now but the terrain wasn't easy. The wind blows the top snow off so a lot of the time we were skiing on ice. Going downhill was tough. With the ice underneath and the wind behind you, you pick up a lot of speed, and with soft boots you don't have a lot of control. Let's just say I fell over a lot.

We went in a big loop around town, then headed for the far mountains and followed the frozen shoreline. The other two were a bit faster than me and after a while were at a bit of a distance. The sight was awesome. The two of them looked so small against their surroundings and the mountains put into perspective the vastness of land we were in. The twilight sun was peering through the clouds and the loose snow chased the horizon riding on the bitter winds. It created a sort of moving blanket over the ground. It would have made the most brilliant picture but sadly I didn't have my camera.

We've been doing dogsledding 101 style, learning what to do and what not to do with the sleds. How to handle the dogs. How to harness them. How to take care of them. The commands necessary while running the dogsleds. We did that in the morning for two or three hours, and then in the afternoon we went cross-country skiing for two or three hours, to acclimatise ourselves to the weather, to figure out what clothing combinations work best for us, and to try to button down all our gear. By the time we leave on Thursday we want to be ready. Today we combined our skiing and the dogsledding, meaning that when the dogs are running and pulling the loaded sled, the driver stands on a platform behind and the other member of the team skis alongside the sled. On the flat parts and the fast parts you can hang on with one hand to the sled itself, and with the other hand we rigged, more or less, a ski tow rope in front, and you ski alongside the sled. You always have to shuffle your feet, otherwise the extra weight can tire the dogs out over the course of the day. On uphill parts, we have to push the sled uphill, which can be tricky when you're wearing skis. It's hard work, though maybe not as much for Ed – he's used to running up mountains.

After three hours we got back. I was exhausted and needed a sit down. I'm glad I've got this training before I start. It's going to be vital.

Tonight I'm sleeping in Otto's room to get a proper rest, away from the crowded room and the late-night gossiping, so I will be on fighting form tomorrow to seize another day.

Sunday 22 April

We woke up at around 8.00 a.m. and headed over to base camp for our daily meeting. There are about five kids here from the School of Environmental Studies, Minnesota. They've organised an exchange with some of the kids from Clyde River. After the meeting I went around the town and was filmed asking people, mainly children, if they had heard of global warming and what they knew about it. Their answers were surprising. They were very aware of the effects of global warming on their culture and environment. It seems to be a regular part of the school syllabus – and even here, where they have a very low carbon impact, they find ways to reduce it further. Are schoolchildren elsewhere as aware as this? I think the difference is that, even in the settlements where things are modernising, the Inuit live so close to the land and are so much a part of nature, that the smallest change is instantly noticed. The adults talk about the whales coming earlier – or not coming at all; of the seals not finding enough ice platforms to give birth and build their snow dens; of birds coming earlier; of bergs breaking up faster – there are so many things that influence their daily lives they have to take note of, whereas we 'Southerners' are sheltered from most of the problems of basic survival in the raw.

In the afternoon we went out driving the dogs again. This time we drove John's dogs, which are a lot more temperamental as there are a lot of alphas in the group, but they are better runners. There was a top layer of fresh snow and the terrain seemed even more beautiful. Tying the dogs up again froze my fingers – it's frightening how instantaneously the cold bites – so I think I'm going to have to wear warmers. These are a very useful invention consisting of little packets of powder which, when shaken, miraculously produce heat through a chemical reaction. You put them inside your gloves and they certainly warm up your hands quickly. In the evening we went over to the teacher's house for dinner. We watched a video on the history of the settlements; it is a very tragic story.

In the 1950s the Canadian government decided that as the Arctic was Canadian, they needed to populate as much of it as possible. The only people capable of doing this were the 'Eskimos'. The government chose certain people from certain families and told them they would be moved to places with better animals to hunt and they could return whenever they wanted. As the families were broken up people were crying. Once on the ships heading up to the deep Arctic, the families realised that it would be hard to go home.

The lands they were placed in were barren and not much wildlife resided there, but few could afford to pay to go home. Nearer to Canada, 'Eskimos' were told their way of life was ancient. Children were taken away from their mothers by the Catholic Church and forced to learn the 'white' ways in school. A lot of them were allegedly molested, treated badly and most lost their culture and the ability to live off the land as they had done happily for the last 5,000 years. They were not even allowed to speak their native language, so when they returned home they struggled to communicate with their families. All this was new to me. I knew of the suffering of other people, moved because they were inconvenient. The Native Americans on the Trail of Tears when they were forcibly marched to reservations; I had seen the rabbit-proof fence that told of how Australian Aborigines were relocated and the children split from their families. I had known first hand of the African diaspora, when tribal lands were lost to white settlers. But somehow, I had never thought of people of the Arctic as suffering in the same way. To me, they were just 'the people of the Arctic' – mysterious, stable, unchanging – as old and as wise as the land itself.

I found a book, *The Long Exile*, by Melanie McGrath, lying around base camp and dipped into it. It describes some of the almost unrelenting horror of this forced relocation on one group, who in 1959 were dumped on a narrow beach on Ellesmere island, just off Greenland when 'the frail summer had already begun to sicken and the sky pressed down on the land like a dead hand'.

At 81 degrees north latitude, Ellesmere is the harshest terrain that humans have ever continuously inhabited. Its interior is an impenetrable mass of frozen crags and deep fjords. The Inuit soon learned that marine mammals were scarce, as were caribou, fox and fresh water. It was 30 degrees colder than it had been back home, and the wind chill made it 50 degrees colder. Their clothing wasn't warm enough, and their sleds wouldn't run on the rocky terrain. The rough waters made hunting by kayak impossible, and the dry wind made their dogs' lungs bleed. The snow blew off the high arctic desert and there wasn't enough to build igloos, leaving the settlers in flimsy canvas tents until late winter. They hadn't brought enough oil for fires and couldn't hunt for enough supplies of blubber. Four months of darkness 'made hunting an almost daily terror'.

There was nothing there – no other group they could be absorbed into, no traditional knowledge of migratory routes, where seals and caribou were, the best fishing grounds, the sea's eddies and currents, the direction of the winds. In fact, there were no caribou, just a small herd of protected muskox, huge and dangerous creatures they weren't allowed to hunt. They didn't know where to look for willow or berries, or which rivers they could fish for char.

They felt abandoned, betrayed and disorientated. They had been told they could leave after a year if it didn't work out, but when they eventually lost their natural reticence and complained, their passage home was refused. It is the Inuit way to not express feelings, whether rage, lust or ambition, because complainers, it was thought, fractured and threatened group survival. In fact, people who did complain were banished. Their unwillingness to speak out on Ellesmere would almost kill them. Unable to find enough seal to feed themselves let alone their dogs, their dogs starved and died. People starved too. They ate bird feathers and made broth from boot liners. One little girl of six had to go hunting seals by herself, on the ice in total darkness, to feed her sick family.

The book describes how, as the years wore on, the Inuit gradually learned how to survive on Ellesmere. They constructed huts from scrap wood, built different kinds of sleds and dog harnesses. They learned the beluga whale's migration route. They asked for a schoolteacher for the children – one came, bringing only two school books: one on how to run a bank, the other called 'The Roads of Texas'. Forty years later, the Canadian government called this relocation 'one of the worst human rights violations in the history of Canada'.

What did surprise me was how little the people blamed anyone. They seemed quite stoical. Some of it is their natural culture of not apportioning blame – but perhaps some of it is that those with long memories are dying out and a younger generation is coming through, so the grief is not as prominent as it was even ten or twenty years ago. I think they were quite welcoming to us because we do react and want to know more. People like Will and the others listen to their wisdom and do not take advantage of them.

Theo told us how something similar happened to him. He was taken from his mother to be schooled. After seven years his brother came and took him out and retaught him his culture and natural ways of living. He speaks with a little resentment but is forgiving. The beauty of it is that the Inuit are not angry at the 'white man' as individuals; they don't seem to generalise.

It is fascinating to me how people survive here, let alone how they survived here 5,000 years ago!

After dinner I headed to the house of the guy who owns the local store. I met with Otto and Daryl and we had a few drinks. Alcohol out here is restricted and hard to get hold of. I think it's limited to two bottles a month for people from outside and illegal for Inuits – it reacts badly with them because of their genetic make-up. The Inuit originally came to the Arctic from Asia, and fifty per cent of Asians are unable to process alcohol, something which has been inherited by the Inuit (as well as by Native Americans). They experience toxic reactions, including headache, nausea, vomiting and hypotension, while a few can get deeply depressed and suicidal. It's important to stress that it was the Inuit themselves who decided to pass this law after some bad experiences.

Tonight I'm sleeping in a tent camped about half a mile from base. John Huston is training me how to sleep out in the Arctic – I have never slept in snow before, let alone in the Arctic Circle. It is definitely all about routines and checks out here. Forget them at your own peril. When sleeping you have to make sure you are in a perfect position. You can't breathe in your bag because your breath freezes and causes ice, which will make your bag wet. Some of the expedition members get dressed and undressed inside their sleeping bags and roll up their clothes as a pillow to keep it all warm. Knitted caps are worn, and the hood of the sleeping bag pulled up close. It sounds complicated but you need to be alert all the time to avoid getting frostbitten. The wind is howling outside and I can picture in my head the vastness around me. It's mad to think I'm sleeping on the sea.

Stetson - as everyone calls him - insists that we always travel in pairs at all times when we're on these short trail trips outside of town, so we won't get lost. He jokes sometimes - when we were just half a mile away - saying, 'People are asked to come and find us if we don't return.'

He told us that one of his jobs on the last leg coming into Clyde River was to act as trail sweep, leaving no signs that dog teams and their crews had ever passed by.

The task of trail sweep was to pick up odds and ends that fell off the back of sleds. The dogs would see these dark objects up ahead in the white snow - hey, could be good to eat! The dogs picked up speed, anticipating a good snack. But it was usually gas bottles, Simon's parka (more than once), hats, masks, rope, knives, a whip. The dogs were always disappointed - except once, when two frozen fish fell off a sled. Fish and bread and small last-minute items were stuffed in between bigger packs anywhere on the sled. 'Hey! Fish escaping,' Stetson yelled. The dogs pounced on one and ate it. Stetson saved the other to eat later. To him it was always bittersweet to leave the trail and come into civilisation. The trail was very simple. Eat, sleep, travel - eat, sleep, travel. But when he saw the warm welcome from this kind and friendly people, he was always glad to be amongst them.

Afterwards, all this - doing chores in a storm, feeding the dogs, packing up, moving off - seems a dream when I'm back at base, reading a book in the warmth of a building.

Monday 23 April

Sleeping in the tent last night was OK. Once you get a routine down it all seems not too tough. I managed to go to the loo twice (in my pee bottle) with no trouble so that's one less thing to worry about. Once in your sleeping bag you don't want to get out until morning, so a pee bottle is an essential bit of equipment. I only woke up once and with the light found it hard to get back to sleep, but only for a little while. It's funny, the two dreams I remember consisted of me pissing myself and being attacked by a polar bear. Who says dreams aren't linked to things going on in your life!

We woke up at 7 a.m. and the wind was howling. Snow had covered the base of the tent and the sun was up and full. It wasn't too cold inside the tent but once out of your sleeping bag your clothes need to go on quickly. One uncomfortable thing is that the condensation that builds up overnight freezes on the inside of the tent. As you move around in the morning it falls on you and your sleeping bag. Apart from that and my frozen breath on my bag, my first night sleeping out in the Arctic was a success.

I had felt no sense of isolation out on the ice, and only little frissons of fear when there were strange sounds in the night – your thoughts do turn to polar bears and wolves. When people asked if I was lonely in that vast and windy wilderness, I could honestly say, no – I loved it. Some people might find being away from civilisation and a fast way of life strange – but I'm very comfortable in that environment and living for the moment. I entered into the spirit of the terrain and felt at peace. In a strange way, it was similar to being in the Caribbean, where there are vast spaces around you, the sea and the sky, and nothing else. This sea up here is frozen and cold, but you get the same sensation and perspective, clear-headed and deep. Instead of grains of sand, there are granules of snow. Both are isolated white beaches.

The 9 a.m. meeting happened as usual but I had to leave early to interview one of the elders, which was filmed for the National Geographic documentary (perhaps you can catch it when it's aired). After speaking to the elder and others, I am realising that it is not the Inuit that need help, it is us.

The Inuit have been adapting to their surroundings for centuries. For anyone to be able to live in this sort of environment you have to know it well. Whatever changes the Inuit face, they will survive because they know and understand the land. Can we say the same for us? We cannot help ourselves if we do not know our planet. If changes occur, can we adapt well enough to survive?

After the meeting I interviewed Hugh Brody, an anthropologist who has been coming out here since 1971. I can't tell you all he told me – it would fill a book – but watch his film *The Eskimos of Pond Inlet*. He describes them as hunter-gatherers, people who live off and on the land in the traditional self-sustaining way. Having spent time with the Inuit in the early 1970s and 80s, Hugh saw many good things about a way of life that has started to vanish. He travelled with dog teams, ventured in the snow and even lived in igloos. Living and working with the Inuit people, he reversed the colonial relationship whereby the Inuit way of life is considered ignorant, and instead he asked the Inuit to teach him about their ways. He speaks several languages and learned two Inuktitut dialects. Language, he told me, is the key to understanding cultures. It reveals different ways of knowing the world. He talked about the legendary fact that Inuktitut has 347 words for snow and elaborated that hunter-gatherer language has very specific words such as 'snow that has recently fallen' or 'snow that is falling through the air', 'snow that has been driven in the wind' and so on. They are all pieces of information about the environment. Being with the Inuit gives you a sense of being with the most gracious, generous and sophisticated of human beings. Far from being simple, they are very, very rich and complex.

After lunch at the hotel, John, Ed and I went out driving. I've got the knack of the dogs down and am really enjoying it. I no longer expect them to eye me up for their dinner. It was our first day skiing alongside and I didn't find it too tough. Ten hours a day, though, and I'm sure I'm going to be exhausted. I hope my back doesn't play up. (I was in a car crash when I was ten, and when I'm extra stressed my back and neck ache, but it doesn't stop me doing what I want.) You have to go to the loo while moving so that's going to be interesting!

This evening we went to the local community centre to watch some competitions. The suicide rate in these areas is high, as there is a real sense of detachment from any sort of culture. I think the youth here have a major loss of identity, and as their environment and way of life change more rapidly, the problem becomes magnified. They are stuck between traditional and modern and some don't seem to be handling it well. The idea that the suicide rate is so high here amongst the youth shocked me. It never crossed my mind that they would have the same kind of problems as the kids in cities. For most Western kids, it's a struggle to try to thrive in the city. An awful lot of people are just trying to get by in life. The biggest threat to sixteen to eighteen year olds in England is the risk of suicide. The rate is high and the reasons varied – overcrowding, competition, fear of failure, bullying, even loss in love. But I find it hard to understand in the Arctic. I asked why – and the explanation I was given makes sense. I was told that the kids are losing their identity in the changing environment. In the past the people had so much to do – just surviving was a full-time job – that they didn't have time to dwell on anything. Boys learned at a young age how to hunt, going out with the men; while the girls were taught other skills, like fishing, making clothes and melting blubber. Now, they watch television all the time – mainly MTV – and they feel a mixture of boredom through lack of exercise and a desire to have all the good things that they see the MTV generation having. They rely on modern food more. Many live on the compensation the government gave their families for relocating them, so they have money, but they can't spend it on the things kids crave after watching so much TV, like fast cars and going out.

A group of break-dancers have taught the children as a way of channelling their thoughts and energy and it has helped a lot. They were bloody good. The children here are so friendly. They all run up to you and say, 'What's your name?' because it's not frequent that outsiders visit. Anyone new in town is exciting so they usually put on events to entertain guests – and themselves, too.

The Clyde River hip-hop dancers brought the house down. The group of twenty or so, most between the ages of six and twenty, spun, flipped, kicked and 'popped' to the driving beat. A crowd of 150 people looked on, cheering, smiling, nodding to the rhythm and gasping at some of the more acrobatic feats. Dancing has been part of Inuit culture for centuries. Kilaujaq, the traditional drum dance of the Arctic, is an excellent example of this. I asked Marie Airut (wife of Lukie Airut, one of the hunters who is hitting the trail with us) for an elder's perspective on the dances. 'Square dance, hip-hop, drum dance, it's all the same ... to be happy with other people,' she explained. 'When we want to have a good time, or be with other people, we dance. Kilaujaq is something we do for special occasions if we want to celebrate something. We invite people into a huge igloo for a big drum dance. In my culture only the man plays the drum (known as a qilaut) and the ladies sing the song ... aye ya ya. I know how to sing this song.'

I sat and played and laughed with the kids for hours. A lot of them are very beautiful and so kind and gentle. One of them asked, 'Are your eyes real?' I don't think it's often that they see blue eyes. One thing I will remember them saying is, 'Who is your girlfriend?' I would point at different girls and they would laugh for hours. They never grew tired of it!

The documented effects of melting permafrost in recent decades have had a direct impact on the Clyde River community. In 1999, the school made headlines across the north as a portion of the structure started to sink into the melting permafrost. Studies show that the temperature of the permafrost has risen by two degrees in the Clyde River region. This also has an effect on lakes and rivers, which begin to dry up, as the less-frozen ground becomes more porous. Roads and houses begin to buckle and lean. Residents here have expressed their concern and worry that the whole town may need to be moved in the near future if the warming trend continues. In some regions, there is little fresh water, thanks to no snow falling for some years – even though they are surrounded by sea ice, they have to sink wells to get unsalted drinking water.

There's a lot to take in all the time. The children here seem to be constantly aware of their history and tradition and their need to survive in a modern world. The Inuit language is still strong here. They primarily use Skidoos but they have dog teams as well. Even though the children don't need to know all the traditions, the elders teach them about their history and language. Elko Antutiqjuak said, 'We want to teach traditional sewing skills, using seal and caribou skins, and what animal skins to wear in certain seasons. We want to teach students about kayaks and boat build-ing, and about the wide variety of specialised tool that Inuit use.'

Many of the younger generation are unemployed and depend on their grandparents for support. If they know their culture they can sew or carve or hunt. With these skills, they can become independent and confident. Igah, another elder, talked of climate change with sadness but determination. 'I've noticed the world has really changed,' he said. 'I used to go for walks and it was the perfect temperature. Nowadays the sun is really hot. We can't rely on technology alone to survive. We need to teach our children how to live on the land.' They even decided to try to raise money to install wind and solar power. It was great to hear how forward-thinking they were, in this small settlement deep within the Arctic Circle.

After I had a meeting with the film team about ideas, Mickey, the director of the film we're doing, arrived. He's a black South African guy with dreads. He seems on it and looks like he wants to go in a good creative direction.

Bedtime soon and I'm looking forward to not worrying about my breath freezing!

Tuesday 24 April

The day has wound to an end and the sun is slowly setting outside. I woke up this morning after a deep sleep. By night-time here you are so exhausted. Not only is it nonstop but the cold takes it out of you. This morning we had our 9 a.m. meeting as usual. It's nearing launch day and things are getting busy. Mickey spoke to the team and gave them

▲ Father and son embarking on an adventure together
  - with me showing Dad the ropes for a change!

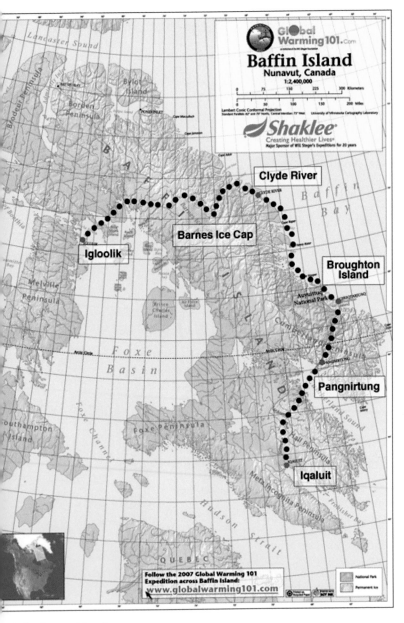

Our long, cold route . . .
(Courtesy of the Will Steger Foundation/Jim Paulson)

▲ Our first night at camp - adrift at sea!   ▼ The Kings and Queens of the Arctic

▲ Simon teaching me how to build an igloo

▼ It's just like very cold Lego – honest!

◀ You'd better trust your roofer – Simon and me testing our igloo

▼ Simon says . . . we deserve a lie down in our Arctic living room

▲ This captures some of the beauty of the place. If you look closely you can see a glacier in the background

▼ Winter wonderland - an edge of the Barnes Ice Cap. You can literally see the years that have passed

▲ A receding glacier - the lines on the right show how big the glacier used to be

◄ Dad and Simon - one joker meets another. The icicle is probably older than both their ages added together!

◀ Never-ending skies

◀ A well-earned rest – it's a dog's life!

◀ Surrounded by mountains – I can't
explain how small it makes you feel!

an idea of what he wants the film to be. After a long meeting we had a ten-minute break and then started organising our food rations for the weeks ahead.

Our breakfast consists of granola and oats. Lunch is carbo bars, soup and nuts along the way and dinner is a mix of pasta or rice. Somehow, we have to eat a block of butter a day to keep our energy levels up. This is burned off over the course of the day keeping your body warm. During Will's eight-month expedition crossing Antarctica, despite eating a block of butter a day his cholesterol level actually dropped. Most people melt it into their granola or pasta, etc., but some eat it by itself. No thanks! There's lots of cheese to be eaten, which I'm happy about. Also we have raw caribou and fish, and may hunt along the way. After a manic organising of mine and Dad's box, we sat down for another logistical meeting. It is hard enough to plan our expedition to ensure the sleds aren't overloaded for the dogs' sake, but there is the film crew to organise with Skidoos, equipment, food and outfits from Iglulik. We'll basically be travelling two people per sled and we arrange our gear so that the bulk of our personal stuff goes in a large duffel. Our sleeping bags and mattresses are in a large nylon sack, called a bivvy sack, which is laid on top of the sleds. There's so much to do and I find it fascinating how it is all carried out. If one thing is forgotten it can all go horribly wrong.

This afternoon Simon and I went to build an igloo. Simon is a great guy with a true sense of humour. He knows this environment very well and I feel safer having him on this expedition. He killed his first polar bear when he was six. This evening I interviewed another elder and learned some more about this place. He used to be in the army and taught the Canadian troops how to survive in the Arctic environment. Otto was filming us, moving his position so he could focus on the elder who was speaking, or me, who was listening. A potentially embarrassing moment came when Otto was behind the elder, looking at me in the viewfinder. I was concentrating hard, trying to look interested while also trying to understand some of his pronunciation, which at times was a little difficult – and there must have been something about my expression that started Otto off in a fit of giggles. I started to giggle, then schooled my face, but when Otto burst out laughing at my struggles, there was that awful moment when you know you're not supposed to laugh and it makes you laugh even more. Then you can't stop. Anything seems funny – even trying to stop laughing is hysterically funny. I thought of the theatrical term – corpsing – when people on stage get a fit of the giggles and try to cover it up by schooling their expressions into a frozen mask – and that struck me as funny, and I laughed even harder. It was infectious – and the elder found it funny himself. The people here never find it hard to laugh. It's very refreshing.

This evening we went to the community centre again and the kids were as mad as ever. At any one time there's about ten kids around you. They always run straight up and say, 'What's your name?' Again and again they say, 'Who's your girlfriend?' and they burst out laughing. It makes me think about my friends and girlfriend. Things are nonstop here and I don't think about the outside world much. I am always truly in the moment unless I'm thinking about them. They would love the children here and I wish they could see this spectacular place.

I found out today that John Stetson's wife, Shelly, is battling with cancer. She made him carry on with this expedition and it shows how important this project is and how dedicated these people are to it. I can really feel myself drawn in. I have formed an emotional attachment and I love the Inuit culture. This is definitely something that I really enjoy and it will only be the start for me. It incorporates a lot of what I love: nature, wildlife, people, sport, challenges, extremes and many other dynamics of life. I have only scratched the surface but I have already learned so much. I have definitely got the bug and it's addictive! I am looking forward to getting home and sharing my knowledge. It is something I can truly speak passionately about and I hope people might learn something from my experiences.

Tonight I was meant to have a meeting with Will but we missed each other. I want to chat with him about how he thinks my role in all this could work and what I can do to help.

Pen's going down and I'm off to my sleeping bag. I can't wait. I just wish I could snuggle up to my beautiful girlfriend, smell her hair and feel the warmth of her skin. When I'm home again I'll be looking forward to it.

Wednesday 25 April

Usual 9 a.m. meeting. Launch tomorrow and everything is slowly slotting into place. After I had an interview with CBC (Canadian Broadcasting Corporation) news and a local paper about myself and the expedition, then I finished packing and headed out with Simon and Ed to feed the dogs and learn the Inuit calls. I love the way the dogs are so alert and instantly responsive, tails wagging, eyes bright, ready to do as I ask. It doesn't give me a sense of power – more a sense of mutual trust and communication. Inuit dogs look after their 'musher' and always bring him home.

This afternoon Dad arrived. I felt very happy to see his broad grin and familiar face. I felt quite chuffed because I'd been out here first;

and although this started out as his project, I felt in a way that it had become mine. Dad has done so many madcap stunts all his life – most of them on his own – and this was great to be sharing something and to be spending time with him. At times I find it hard to grasp all of the things that Dad has done. He was racing across the Atlantic in huge stormy seas when he got the news of my birth. So even as he won the Blue Riband trophy, he had the bonus of my arrival (he says)! We've shared a few adventures. Dad even spent time with me on my gap year in Australia when I taught him to surf, which was cool.

Hugging him on his arrival in the Arctic was a different experience for both of us. The adventure we were about to launch ourselves on wasn't life threatening and we had a fantastic, strong team around us – but it was something new to have me telling him how to survive for once. I think I'm now hitting the age where it's slowly turning around. As everyone knows, it happens at some point – and Dad jokes about it. We've both got a long way to go before we hit the middle ground on equal footing though and I'm in no rush. I have many miles to go. But it's good to have him here and I've been trying to cram my training and what I've learned in the last few days into his head in a couple of hours. In a way, I'm glad I came out here first and made my own mark. Dad's arm is still not fully healed from when he had an accident with a quad bike in Spain, and he isn't sure how he'll be skiing, especially over this kind of terrain. It's not like downhill skiing, where your legs and torso do most of the work – in the Arctic, you have to use your whole body, including your arms. I've told him that he can ride on the sled and we'll tuck him in and look after him!

The students at Quluaq School in Clyde River have something to say to the world: 'We love our land!'

The children drew pictures of their homeland and native traditions during the expedition team's visit to the school today. Included in the drawings were pictures of igloos, dogsleds, kayaks, tents and inukshuks as well as images from the Arctic landscape. The students had very clear ideas about how global warming affected their home. Will and Abby were moved and said they'd deliver several of the drawings to the US Senate during their presentation in July. The team also dropped in on the high school, where the students there had a message to deliver, in English and Inuktitut: a list of Clyde River's 101 'Solutions to Pollution' for our Earth.

> Live like an Inuit, simple and off the land
> Skidoo less and walk or dogsled more
> Instead of using motorboats, canoe, kayak and sail
> Eat more raw foods

Will thought that the 101st solution on the list was a universal message for people around the globe: 'Educate yourself ... read as much as you can on global warming and share with your children ... for their future ...' I thought it was a good message.

This evening we went to the community hall for a thank-you/good-bye feast. Chopped up raw meat and fish was on a tarpaulin on the floor. It was fascinating to watch these kids with bomber jackets on and AC/DC hats eating raw meat off the floor. A real mix of traditional and modern. I tried some of the raw caribou meat, but as it melts in your mouth the taste of blood is quite overpowering.

I sat down with Will and he asked if I would be keen to join him next year on a trip over Ellesmere Island to observe the collapsed and yet-to-collapse ice shelves. It's something I'm going to have to consider seriously.

I have just had my last shower and am off to bed – 6 a.m. start tomorrow and I'd better save some energy. I can't wait to head off. I can't explain but I feel truly in my element. I couldn't wish to be anywhere more awesome. Sleep time.

Thursday 26 April
25 Miles

I'm here at the end of my first day on the trail, sitting in my tent. We're in a beautiful canyon with equally lovely weather.

This morning we woke up and packed our things. We had our meeting and loaded up all the sleds with the gear, then headed off at around 10.30 a.m. The whole town came out to see us off and lots of kids kept saying to me, 'Please don't leave.' It was really touching. One of the teachers from the school gave me a necklace which a partially sighted girl from the school had made for me. It's a carving of an inukshuk in soapstone. It's for good luck and to guide me. Traditionally inukshuk were put around the land to guide the hunters. They are a pile of stones, like a chess piece as tall as a person and, while they all look the same, there is something subtle about their design that passes on a message to travellers.

Setting off was pretty crazy and the dogs were seriously excited. A couple of the sleds headed off without anyone on them. When the dogs want to go they will and there's nothing you can do to stop them. You always have to keep your wits about you. The kids were all asking for my photo and to shake my hand. It was so sweet. I think the blond hair and blue eyes caught their attention!

I started on John's sled, while Dad started with Simon and Theo. Will and Elizabeth were with Luke and Ed was with Abby. Will often switched us about so that we shared sleds and tents with different people. This meant we would get to know each other and share experiences. It was a good system.

Once we had set off properly it took a while for the dogs to calm down. Everyone had a few spills. One time when the dogs bolted I had to reach behind me and grab John and pull him up onto the sled. It was like a scene from *Cliffhanger*.

The sea ice in front of Clyde River was much flatter and smoother than in some other places along the Atlantic coast of Baffin Island. Partly this lack of jumbled ice is due to minimal tides in Clyde River, contrasted with dramatic tidal fluctuations in Iqaluit and other villages further south. We all guessed that our departure from Clyde River would be less chaotic without the jumbled ice barrier to negotiate. Before getting too confident, however, we all tried to remind ourselves that anytime dogs are involved there is potential for some chaos. We did have some new factors playing into the mix; a film crew is joining the expedition for this leg, there are three new team members, and we have several new dogs.

Because Lukie runs his dogs in the traditional Inuit fan-hitch style with long bearded seal traces connecting each dog to a main trace, he has to stop occasionally to untangle the traces. Lukie is quick at doing this. As he untangles them he hands me each one and I thread the carved bone toggle through the main trace. Once all the toggles are threaded through, I fasten the main trace into a loop. This secures all the dogs to the sled.

Today, however, our film crew, still beginning to figure out how to film around dog teams, sped past just at the moment that Lukie had detached all the dogs from the main trace and was holding the tangled mess of leads in his hands. The dogs saw them with all their cameras and gear and instantly gave chase. Lukie held tightly to the knot of traces and dug his heels into the snow, but he was no match for the fourteen eager dogs. They pulled Lukie like a barefoot water-skier. I had two dogs' traces in my hands and soon flew after him.

The film crew realised what was happening and stopped. The dogs, Lukie and I caught up to them where, luckily for us, the dogs also stopped. We held them tightly as Will brought the sled up from behind. Lukie quickly finished untangling the traces and I reconnected them with haste to the main trace. The film crew are quick learners and by the end of the day they were working out how to film our sleds without causing too much havoc.

We expect to have at least one more day on the sea ice before we reach the end of the fjord. If the temperatures stay relatively cool, we should make good time. At midday today, however, it was warm enough that the snow was starting to get soft and mushy. Soft snow can slow down the dogsleds.

As the town fell away into the distance I got my first feeling of real space and wilderness. The most incredible sights are to be seen here. I had my first true expedition experience. What a sight: the sleds in the distance in different directions, vast trails of white off into the horizon with mountainous walls either side of the frozen sea we are travelling on, and the fjord which is leading us inland, pretty much directly from east to west. We've been going west all day, and we made about 25 miles in distance today, as the crow flies, though we travelled about 30 miles in total. It was calm and sunny, perfect conditions for packing the sleds this morning, and also for getting out of Clyde River. The terrain was very good, with lots of flat sea ice. In some areas the ice is snow covered, while in others it's fairly glazed ice, which makes travel quite easy.

Along the way we stopped for some tea and snacks, and when we arrived at a good camp spot, we stopped for the night and organised everything. We unpack the sled, tie the dogs off, feed them, put the tent up, axe some ice, melt the ice for cooking and water for the morning, and dry mukluks and clothes etc. – it would be the same routine every night. This is our first day and we left a little bit later than we had planned. We travelled about eight hours and ended our sledding at around 6 p.m. Normally, we probably would have gone another couple of hours, but this is a bit of a shakedown day, and we're quite happy with the results. It was a terrific day. The sled that I was on, I skied next to, pushed and pulled, so got quite tired by the end. I think we're having arctic char stew tonight – it's a type of salmon that lives up here. In other parts of the world it's very expensive, but up here it's in such abundance that they feed it to the dogs.

Wow, what a stunning place. There are mountains all around and the sea ice is flat. It gives you so much perspective. I think the challenge is to keep that perspective when you go back to the other world. The clarity of thought here is refreshing and it's nice not to have the clutter of everyday life. We unpacked the sled near the tent so the dogs can warn us if any polar bears come. We also sleep with a shotgun, just in case.

Friday 27 April
*25 miles**

This morning we woke up at 5.30 a.m. That gave us just over an hour to get ready. John is very exact about the way things should be done. After some oatmeal and our only bacon we packed up the sleds and filled our bottles for the day.

It was another glorious day and the sun was shining bright. We made some good ground up Clyde Fjord. The two brown puppies that were struggling to keep up on Simon's sled yesterday were let go for a few hours, as I later found out that Simon had planned for them to be picked up if they couldn't keep up.

We are among mountains – and mountaineers. Abby said Ed Viesturs was getting a crash course in mushing, and she was lucky enough to be crashing along with him. After twelve days in the village, our dogs, plus two more, are raring to go. Stopping and starting are often eventful affairs, especially over sea ice with minimal snow. The snow hook pops out of its hold, the dogs take off before you're ready, and your hot cocoa – your only luxury – goes flying through the air. Just for the record, Abby said that Ed was a champ. He took it all in his stride, with the competence and confidence of someone who has climbed Mount Everest (six times!). They covered some ground today, in miles and in conversation. When she asked him how he came to this expedition, he

---

* Some of the distances I give are as the crow flies on the map, while others are actual distances covered by foot and sled.

said it was a toss-up between a seventh trip to Everest or an expedition with Will Steger. Abby grilled him about climbing Everest, and how he got to where he is today. Leaving veterinary medicine wasn't easy, he said, after seven years of school. It took courage to go after a life less secure and predictable. But he's never regretted it and has found a way to make a living doing what he loves.

I was doing something I loved; but I wondered about what I wanted to do with the future. There was plenty of time to think about that. Meanwhile, I was in the middle of three-thousand-foot vertical cliffs. I would be seeing, I think, the best sights on the trip aided by the helpful weather. Huge mountains stood either side of the fjord and we were still sledding over the sea ice. In one corner was a towering cliff with a huge glacier above it. Theo pointed out a glacier that he said used to be five times the size. Up ahead of us, 25 miles of fjords, vertical cliffs and hanging glaciers sparkled in a lovely light as we travelled in the shade to keep the dogs cool. Moving into the shadow of a deep cliff, it felt like winter again, then out into the sun. It is perfect ice conditions for running dogs and they were energised, as we were. Stetson said that he had seen many places in the Canadian Arctic, but this was the most dramatically beautiful.

There was a calm light in the afternoon and Clyde Fjord continued to get more and more spectacular by the mile. We passed mountains and glaciers, huge cliff faces and scree slopes. The sun was warm, almost too warm for our dogs, who were thirsty for snow and ate it when they could. We stopped in a large swath of shade to give them a break. The going was relatively smooth and quick. Tomorrow we will enjoy the last of the flat, fast trail, as we get ready for a climb up towards the Barnes Ice Cap.

We're in camp now, cooking up some dinner, melting ice for water, and things have been going very well. We got here at about 6 p.m., after travelling a little over eight and a half hours today, covering 25 miles as the crow flies. (As with yesterday, we probably travelled 30 miles by winding around through the fjord, on very flat sea ice terrain.) Tonight Otto and I joined Will and Dad in their tent and chatted for a while about the film and its aims. I think the key is to get across the Inuit voice and visually give people something they can form an emotional attachment to. I'm learning so much already and we've only just begun.

What a magical spot to set up camp - surrounded by glaciers and mountains. For two hours a near full moon and quietness (apart from the dogs! Last night they woke me up three times.).

Saturday 28 April
22 miles

Today has to be the highlight of my year so far. What a spectacular experience. We woke up this morning and left the mountainous valley that had been our home for the night. It was a clear morning with not a cloud in the sky and we set off down the sea ice with no problems. There was a chill in the air but as it neared eleven o'clock the temperature was perfect. Stetson said that of all the times he had been coming to the Arctic the last three days have been the best weather. We managed to travel eleven miles in the first two hours and then things slowed down. We came to the very end of the Clyde inlet, where the sea ice on the sea mountains side of the fjord made way for the fresh water of the frozen Clyde River. It was a narrow ribbon about 20 to 40 feet wide, either ice or snow covered, as it wandered its way through the cliffs. The water was the brightest blue and the sun's reflection off the ice was a twilight fairy-tale. The dogs slid around a lot on the ice but managed pretty well. The sad point of the day was that Simon had to take one of his dogs off its leash. She couldn't keep up because she was about to give birth. At the start of the trip, nobody knew this particular dog was expecting pups. Because she was heavily pregnant, Simon decided it was better for her to not be pulling the sled because she could not keep up. She followed slowly behind the team, a few miles behind, resting when necessary, and was able to catch up to the team by the evening.*

As we travelled up the river, huge bulbs of frozen ice protruded from the river's surface. These form when the river freezes and expands. What a sight. We continued through the frozen gully until we came out the top onto a plateau and a frozen lake. It's a lot more work for us and the dogs on land and can be quite dangerous to manoeuvre with all the rocks, especially going down hill. We have about six days of land to cross and I think it's going to get a lot trickier.

We are camped once again after about an eight-hour journey today. We've been fortunate with the weather, not a breath of wind. It's been

---

* After I wrote this, I heard that there was a happy ending to this story. The dog was fed, cared for and made it safely to her final home community in Iglulik to deliver her seven pups.

between zero and ten degrees Fahrenheit all day long. It was pretty cool to be on the Clyde River but now we're on the mainland, camped on a frozen lake, with jagged hills and big boulders all around. I'm now in my tent ready for bed. The weather's turning and the wind has started to blow. I think tomorrow's going to be a lot colder. What a day though – we sucked in the good weather and were lucky to have it over the most pretty part.

Sunday 29 April
20 miles

How lucky. Again the sun was shining and the sky was clear. Everything ran pretty smoothly except for a few mishaps with the dogs. Now we are on the land the going is a lot tougher. The terrain on the uplands is rough, with rocky hills and steep downhill parts and many little frozen rivers and rapids coming out of the bottom of the Barnes Ice Cap – still some distance away – and snaking down into the Clyde River. It's all quite technical and you have to know what you're doing. Running to the front to steer the sleds is not easy. Every so often we come across crevasses. They are hidden holes under a top layer of ice and snow, some around eight feet deep. They can be dangerous so you have to be alert.

Theo was the first to point out the Barnes Ice Cap in the distance. At first it was barely distinguishable from the snow-covered hills in front. The most noticeable difference was that it seemed smoother and more uniform. As we drew closer, however, the magnitude of the ice cap became clearer to us. Its walls were hundreds of feet high. Their bare ice shone blue in the midday sun. At first the vertical walls seemed impenetrable. We knew, however, that local people regularly travel this route between Clyde River and Iglulik and that there must be a way to mush dog-teams onto it.

We're now skirting around the Barnes Ice Cap, fifteen miles away. Even at that distance, it's a huge, awesome chunk of ice, 75 miles long and 30 miles wide. Just a huge block of ice – a remnant of the last great Ice Age that covered all of Canada and ran far down into what is now the USA. It rises up to 3,000 feet. Will looked keenly ahead, excited. He said, 'I have always wanted to see the Barnes Ice Cap ever since I was a kid.'

I felt really lucky to have stumbled across it at such a young age. It's like looking at history – and I wonder how much longer it will still be there.

Even though it was 29°F (-5°C), the polar Eskimo dogs overheated. Stetson said we might have to start running a midnight shift. It's not as bad as it sounds in the 24-hour sun we now have. It would be light enough to see across this perilous terrain, but it would wreck the schedule. If overcast, the temperature is not too bad; but the sunlight in early May is a dangerous time for ultraviolet rays. The ozone hole is more obvious in higher latitudes, and there's more UV. Later the hole closes but, right now, we have to take care and cover up.

We were managing the long traverses over hilly valleys, with a few steep hills and rocks to veer around. But all was good – until a mishap, when the line snapped on Abby and Ed's sled at the top of a steep hill. The dogs went running and it all went a bit out of control. This is Abby's report.

It happens to every musher, eventually, when you least expect it. One minute you're fine, next thing you know you've lost your dog team. Nine times out of ten, it's due to human error (a fray in the cord, an open carabiner, a poor hold with a snow hook, something missed or neglected). Today it was a rock; one big, buried, beastly rock that stopped our sled dead in its tracks on the steepest slope we've seen since Auyuittuq National Park.

We had been cruising along at a good clip all morning, gradually climbing up out of the Clyde River drainage. The river wound through small canyons, pale blue where the wind had blown the snow away. We followed the frozen trail uphill from lake to lake, admiring the rocky landscape and red rock walls. It was midway through the day when we came to the crest of a tall rise with a large lake stretched out below us. Stetson and Sam were the first to go, followed by Simon and Richard, then Lukie and Will. Ed and I pulled up to assess the scene. Throwing two snowmobile belts over our runners for extra friction, we took our skis off, and started the steep descent. The heavy sled quickly picked up speed and we held on tight to the stanchion.

Then it happened. One minute we were moving, next thing we knew we were at a complete stop. Ed went flying (landing safely in the deep snow below) as I rammed my stomach into the wooden handlebars. The dogs, for their part, were gone.

It's quite a sight, let me assure you, to see ten dogs galloping away at full speed, attached to one another and nothing else, down the trail. I stared for a second in disbelief, then in horror, then in slight panic. Then I was after them ... post-holing, tripping, sprinting through the deep snow, down the hill after them.

One lunge and I missed them. A second lunge and I had the end of the tattered gangline in my hands. Stopping a team of ten dogs, however (who are quite comfortable pulling a hundred pounds each at this point in the trip, when you weigh only one hundred and thirty), is no easy task. I yelled and dragged, and finally got them to stop in a tangled bundle of fur and rope. By this time Ed had made it down the hill as well and together we pulled the growling ball apart.

Thirty yards above us, our sled sat abandoned at the top of the rise. Just when we were wondering how the heck we were going to get down without losing our team again in the process, the film crew pulled into view to save the day. Soon it was all hands on deck, tying new lines, straightening dog harnesses and bringing the sled down to the team. Before long everything was in its place and we were off again, adrenaline the only remaining trace of the fiasco. All's well that ends well.

We travelled hard today, covering over twenty miles in deep snow and warm sun. Our dogs are tired from travelling in the heat and are grateful for any shade we can give them. Our faces are pink and ruddy from facing south, despite covering up as best we could with sunscreen and visors. Tomorrow we continue our ascent towards the much-anticipated Barnes Ice Cap. We had a few stops to rest the dogs and then Lukie discovered he had lost his seal – for the dogs (don't ask!) – and we had to stop for him to retrieve it. After a couple of lunch stops, one to cut up Lukie's seal, we finally made it into the late-night camp. We need to keep pushing high energy food into our bodies to keep up this punishing pace.

After setting everything up (which I've nearly got down) Will, Dad and I chatted and were filmed discussing global warming. It's going to affect my generation more than anyone, so we need to act, to have a voice. With that we can have the power to put pressure on government and politicians to do something about it.

In camp in the evening, I discussed the art of sledding with Ed, who's a sledding novice like me. He agreed that it was quite technical. He said, 'I'm no expert, but the first five miles was probably the hardest of the day. We had to push and pull and get the sleds up the hills and rolls, and they weigh about eight hundred pounds, with two people on each sled. It was exhausting.'

We pushed it to make up for the several stops and got into camp later than usual at about 7.30 p.m. We started the day at around 8.30 this morning, so it was an eleven-hour day, to cover twenty miles over complicated terrain. I could see why Stetson said that dogs are amazing creatures. They pull their hearts out every day. We felt bad because we normally stop at five and this time, after we stopped briefly and then told them to mush again, they looked back as if to say, 'You're having a laugh!'

When they saw we were continuing, they carried on uncomplaining, pulling our huge loads, their legs working in conjunction. Stetson – who loves his dogs with the tender heart of a father – said, 'Dogs are what makes it possible.'

He explained to me the merits of Alaskan husky versus Canadian husky. The Alaskan's short hair is better for heat. It can be too warm for Canadians (like now, though it's 10°F, which I think is pretty damn cold). All the dogs have names and you get fond of those you work with, especially the lead dogs. There's Jones, a ten-year-old veteran and Stetson's favourite dog, who Stetson was concerned about when, during the short sprint from Generator Lake and down the other side, he noticed that the dog seemed off colour. He wasn't hungry for his supper last night, but ate a little bit of fish today. He's a good dog, always willing, with blue eyes that seem to watch for that moment when we get up and he can drive us further into the snow, tail wagging. He loves to follow trail and gets restless when confined.

Whisper's the other lead dog, probably the best trained and most intelligent. She's a very good dog with the heart of a leopard, on loan from Stetson's regular dog-racing partner Jamie Nelson. She's a great gee-haw leader and will do almost anything – deal cards, make coffee, scratch your back.

Monday 30 April
26 miles

Today we had long traverses over hills as far as the horizon. The landscape has become somewhat monotonous but I don't mind. We travelled pretty much continuously for the whole ten hours with the ice cap coming in and out of sight. As we drew closer, in the high pressure we're currently enjoying, we felt a cold stiff headwind down from the ice cap, which helped cool the dogs. Our Inuit partners told us that this wind often blows down from there. The chill of the wind contrasted refreshingly with the warmth of the spring sun. If this keeps up, we can do 35 miles a day provided we don't have too many storms.

The closer we drew to the ice cap, the more awesome it became. A fifty-foot wall of ice jutted out of the ground and at the top the snowy mound went as far as the eyes could see. This wall of ice went on for a mile or so in both directions, and was very dramatic. Getting up on the top looked impossible. Apart from wanting to be 'on top of the world, Ma!' Will also wanted us to go up and over to get away from moraine, a heterogeneous mix of rocks and boulders that skirted the tail of the ice cap. The area here is recently glaciated – apparently, 10,000 years or so is recent in geological time – when massive glaciers and ice went down to the US. The rubble of fresh ice and moraine and the little streams running out from the bottom of Barnes shows in a miniature scale what the whole of the US and Canada must have looked like way back then, when it was freshly exposed along the 2,500-mile length of the great Arctic ice sheet. Awesome!

We made a little over 26 miles today, as the crow flies, so probably more like 32 miles distance on land. Once again, we had a spectacular day. Seems like we're being given this gift of phenomenal weather to travel in, clear and cold.

Simon did a little radio broadcast for the schoolchildren and people who are following our progress right across the US and Canada and further afield. It seems incredible that we are right in the middle of this vast and trackless landscape, yet can be in direct touch with the rest of the world. Simon was eloquent when he described the 'blue blue ice'. He talked of the scenery, the signs of global warming, the friendly welcome everywhere, and how he had built snow houses. It was interesting to gain his take on the trip and his observations. As a hunter, he had acute senses. He spotted caribou tracks everywhere, crossing our path, and said he hadn't seen them for a while. It made him feel we were nearing the end of the trail and his home village of Iglulik – although there were many miles and many days still to go.

Almost immediately, in what I had thought of as trackless land, we passed some Inuit hunters on their way back to Clyde River with several butchered caribou on their komatik sleds. They shared some of their fresh meat with us. Country food is a treat!

As we drew closer, however, the magnitude of the ice cap became more clear to us. We stopped for lunch a short distance from the edge of the ice cap where we could admire the blue ice cliffs behind us. Simon decided to hike over to the edge to explore. He unfastened his dogs' traces from his sled so they could follow him. He and his dogs jogged all the way to the edge of the ice cap and he returned to our sleds with a seven-foot-long icicle he had broken off.

He and Dad joked that the icicle was a narwhal tusk. Dad held the icicle on top of Simon's head and Simon pretended to swim like a narwhal. One joker had found another.

After lunch the dog-teams climbed onto the ice cap via a route that, although more accessible than the vertical cliffs, was still quite steep. Finally, we achieved one of our expedition goals. We travelled across the edge for half a day. Lukie would not let us cross the main part of the cap. Even if it would cut the trip by a great distance and be easier travelling, the risk of crevasses was too high. The Inuit never take unnecessary risks. This environment is dangerous enough. What a magnificent thing. It was staggering to see the sheer size of it and to know that I was standing on top of part of the historical record of geological time. It was very sad to think that within my lifetime, if we don't help change things, some of the smaller caps on Baffin Island might be gone forever. If the unthinkable happens, I wonder if people will come and chip little bits off the last of this dinosaur to sell as souvenirs?

It would have been something to have travelled the entire length of the cap, but it was too risky, and just being on it was quite an achievement. We dropped off the other side and were back to rubble and the undulating plateau below; we sledded about another ten miles. All the way to our camp tonight, however, we could catch glimpses of the ice cap receding from view as we turned. Rising in the distance behind foothills in the foreground, it looked almost like the ocean – a soft bluish plain that seemed to stretch off into infinity.

Dad has just heard that he has to leave tomorrow for business – getting out won't be easy! One of the team used the satellite phone to contact Ken Borek Airlines to send a plane. Some of the Inuit outfitters (hunters) we have along with us, who provide logistical support, have gone ahead to scout for a good location for a small plane to land. I'll be sad to see my dad go – we have made a good team and it's been fun. But his arm has given him some problems and – action man that he is! – he hasn't been able to sled and ski as he would like to. Everyone decided that it would be a good time to ponder our legacy and summarise some of our thoughts. Abby summed it all up very neatly, so I'll give her the floor. (Thanks, Abby!)

Our days are full of light and sun. Darkness has left this corner of the Arctic and left us with a lovely lingering dusk through our sleeping hours.

We rise at 5.30 a.m. with sun-filled tents and light our stoves with relative ease. We break a light sweat packing our sleds and harnessing dogs. By noon the sun is as high as it will be in its low arc across the sky, and we are down to one long underwear layer on top. We have swapped our winter hats for ball caps and visors, and reapply sunscreen again and again to our sunburned faces.

In an effort to adapt to the warmer weather, we stop for longer breaks at midday and travel longer in the morning and late afternoon. Today's break came close to 2.00 p.m. We gathered around Lukie's sleds to look at the maps to calibrate our distance. Gathering together as a group like this is somewhat rare, but that much more important with our guest expedition members on board. There are lots of questions to be asked, thoughts to be shared, and opinions to be aired. Today's discussion turned to global warming and public perceptions of the issue.

'What do you tell people who feel overwhelmed by the issue of climate?' someone asked. Theo was the first to respond. 'Take a look at the people of Clyde River,' he suggested. 'Here they are, way up in the Arctic, far away from everybody, but they know about climate change and they're doing something about it.' Theo is right. Many people in Clyde River use energy-saving bulbs, buy recycled products, and support local investment in alternative energy sources. They are doing their small part as individuals to contribute to a bigger movement towards change.

Elizabeth spoke up about the need for hope. 'Currently we lack any comprehensive vision of global warming solutions. Solutions exist but it's easy to get overwhelmed when all we hear in the media is gloom and doom.' She pointed to the expedition as a way to encourage hope and action, but also called for stronger leadership from government and big business.

Richard threw in his two cents, encouraging us all to hold our governments accountable for mandating policies to slow global warming. 'Governments can do this,' he said, 'and they should.' Richard is an excellent example of big business effecting positive social change. His company, Virgin-Atlantic, is pioneering new ground with their own environmental policies, leading the way in the airline industry and industries around the world.

As we mush a little closer to our final destination every day, our thoughts turn more often to the meaning of the expedition. What will our legacy be? Where will we go from here? To Washington DC for starters! But until then ... it's Iglulik or bust. A bright goodnight, Abby.

We switched tent partners again, and for this last night before he leaves, Dad and I are sharing. We set up camp in a huge basin down to the cap. It's a tremendous view. As I write this, I'm just watching the sun setting now over the horizon. Even though it sets, it doesn't go too far below the horizon. There is 24-hour sunlight and the night-time hours are twilight. The full moon is nearing and we are truly in a magical place.

Tuesday ı May
20 miles

Today we woke up to a cloudy sky. The wind was gentle and not too cold. Dad had to leave to fly to the States. Virgin America is launching finally and he needs to be there. It was sad to say goodbye to him. I would have liked to hang out more. I started out here alone and I'm up to the challenge. I'm not leaving until the end. The Inuit outfitters had found what they hoped might be a suitable location, just past the Barnes Ice Cap, for an airstrip and everyone pitched in to pack down the snow and create a makeshift runway. The GPS co-ordinates were provided to the pilot and it was arranged for the Twin Otter plane to arrive just before sunset. Otto decided to leave as well with his film crew, because a few days ago he got sun blindness. The last two weeks of the expedition had been uncharacteristically warm and sunny for this time of the year – but the most dangerous thing was the intensity of the UV radiation. Coupled with that is the highly reflective nature of the snow. Exposure of skin and eyes can be a problem and wearing sunglasses is a must. Because of the bright sun we were experiencing, it was tempting to uncover and enjoy the sunshine – and unfortunately, Otto wasn't wearing glasses for some time while filming, so he could capture better colours and definition. He suffered snow-blindness about four or five days into our trip. It's a painful experience that feels like you have sand in your eyes. He was tent-bound for a couple of days and had to keep his eyes covered.

We left Dad, Otto and the others on the 'airstrip', lonely figures in all that ice and snow, while we headed out. We travelled pretty much non-stop until evening.

I was travelling with Abby today. We got on well – she's a cool chick. We listened to music and had some good chats. At around 4 p.m. we came to the frozen MacDonald River. This is the only route to Iglulik from the top of the mountains, as the land route is too rocky. The deep soft snow in the shaded river gorge made for arduous travel – but worse was to come. Following the others we realised that the ice was very weak. Every now and again we heard big cracks underneath us. It was stomach churning. You don't know if you're overreacting, and you tell yourself you're not. You don't want to make a big fuss because you're with hard-core Arctic explorers – and then suddenly you hear the crack behind you and it sounds like the chill you're getting inside your body coming up behind you. It's sort of chasing you up, moving fast like a living creature. The noise follows you – the sharp snap sends chills up your body and you hope the crack doesn't catch up with your feet. You want to turn around and look, and the chills shiver up your spine but you can't stop – you have to move forward to beat the crack. If you fall in, you're pretty screwed. You can freeze in a few seconds. It's like when you put a drop of water in a freezer and it freezes fast. If you put yourself in this big freezer at under minus 40, you're that small drop – and you freeze quickly.

I didn't know how deep the river was was; deep enough that we'd be swallowed up or swept away under the ice? The fear grows. We'd been told what to do if we do fall in. Someone gets you out while someone else sets up a tent fast and gets all the heaters blasting. You roll in the snow to get the water off – bizarre as it sounds – and then you race into the tent and strip fast, huddle into a duvet and thank God you're not an icicle.

Just then two of our back dogs broke through the ice. I was terrified we'd fall through as well. We've all jumped in a cold swimming pool and jumped out without touching the sides. They jumped out quickly with the pull of the other dogs and the momentum carried us over without falling through. As we came to the bank and onto the land a sigh of relief came to me. But as we rode round the next corner we saw Simon's sled break through the ice. Elizabeth was sitting on top and half the sled was under water. After a bit of a skirmish, we managed to use Lukie's dogs and a long line to pull them out. A lot of the equipment went in the water, including my bag. Luckily most of it was OK. Will's bag containing all his clothes was soaked through and his down sleeping bag was wet. His reaction was surprising. He just said, 'What I'm wearing will last me,' and he didn't really seem that fazed. It just shows how much he must have been through on some of his trips. It reminds me of the stories I have heard about his epic eight-and-a-half month crossing of Antarctica.

The Macdonald River is known for this. It's constantly got running water through it, which makes it a bit unstable. Not that reassuring, as I'm lying on it now about to go to sleep! Elizabeth is busy in her tent, writing up the story of her adventure today for Global Warming 101 Despatches – and she said I could share it with you, exactly as she set it out. It reads well!

```
Co-ordinates: 69.41.118 N, 74.07.384 W
Distance Travelled: 18.42mi / 29.64km
Weather: Temp 13°F / –10°C, Wind 0 MPH / 0 KPH
Cloud cover: Full Sun
```

Falling through thin ice

Simon calmly turned around to me and said, 'They should not be out there. They are going to sink.' I looked behind me to see Stetson and Ed Viesturs mushing out onto the lake we had just reached. Simon and Lukie's sleds had been the first to arrive at the lake and the two men had cautiously ventured out onto the ice to check it with their harpoons. They returned with an ominous look on their faces that said we would be skirting the edge of the lake instead of crossing it. The past six days of full sun and temperatures hovering just below freezing had taken its toll on the ice and remaining snow.

Just now, however, the word about the thin ice hadn't reached back to Stetson's sled. I turned around and motioned to them with my arms that they should get closer to shore. Stetson called 'Haw! Haw!' to his lead dogs and Whisper and Jones responded immediately, turning the team towards shore and bringing Stetson and Ed to safer ice.

Simon and I continued on the ice, hugging the shore. The shrinking snow-cover on the land had exposed lots of sharp rocks that would damage the soft plastic shoes on Simon's runners if he mushed over the tops of them, so he decided to stay on the ice, but stay close enough to the shore to be safe.

This plan was working well until we reached a small inlet and, instead of hugging the shore, Simon's lead dogs tried to cut across to the opposite bank. We heard a ripple of cracks spread out from under our sled and then felt the sickening feeling of the sled punch through the ice.

Simon yelled to his dogs to pull and the dogs tried, but they soon plunged through the thin ice as well. The top of the sled floated just above the surface of the water.

Simon crawled over to the shore where Lukie and the other sleds were stopped. Quickly Simon and Lukie grabbed a long rope. Simon crawled with the end of the rope back to the sled. He tied the end of the rope to the front of his sled. Lukie untied his dogs from his sled and tied them to the other end of the rope. Lukie's dogs, still on solid ground, were able to pull our dogs and our sled towards shore. The sled ploughed through the ice like an icebreaker, leaving a trail of open water behind it.

Finally the sled drew close enough to shore that I could jump off and help pull the sled to safety. We unpacked the sleds to assess the damage. Will, Simon and Sam Branson's gear was wet. We spent an hour or so wringing out water and spreading clothing out to dry on warm, dark rocks. We then repacked the sled and started again down river.

A few degrees of temperature difference can make a huge impact when those degrees cause a phase change in water. Water is either ice or it is liquid and the change comes quickly when the temperature starts to warm. My brief plunge through the ice made me think about caribou and other animals who rely on ice for travel. I have seen video of caribou trying to migrate over thinning ice and falling through. I have also heard of caribou whose young calves are swept away by strong currents in rivers that, in the past, would have been still frozen during the caribou's migration.

Elizabeth

Today we squeaked out an arduous twenty miles – but it was a bit of an adventure and quite nerve-racking as well. Apart from the mishap in the river, it was difficult travel and we didn't go as far as we had hoped. But, as Will said, we are limited by the strength of the dogs. We can't run them into the ground. We have to let them dictate how far we go in many cases because we still have another seven or eight days to travel to get to the town of Iglulik. But it was, again, a clear and sunny day. Great travel weather and probably 15 to 20°F, which is rather warm for these parts but spring is here, and the warmer temperatures and the sunny skies make it a little harder for the dogs to travel too hard and too fast.

I think I have mentioned before that Stetson is something of a droll joker. At the moment, he's travelling and tenting with Ed Viesturs and, on his live audiocast, Stetson got into a humorous drawling discussion of smelly feet. He said, 'Ed has his same footpads on, Ed's Custom Footpads from the Sole Company. They smell more than mine. But I guess mountaineers sweat more than mushers. Ed has turned out to be very good at mushing, so he might change careers mid-life. He's a non-practising veterinarian and knows a lot about animals.' The audiocast ended in laughter. That's what I like about these people – they're all great fun to be around, like my dad.

I am sharing with Will the next few days. He's quite eccentric in his own way. Bed now. Another long day tomorrow. Forty-five more miles of this river and we don't know how thick the ice will be.

Dad flew over in the plane this evening, and we all mooned him goodbye. I'm on my own now. I am very content and have been alone with my thoughts a great deal. I have real perspective and really feel quite proud. However, my skin is starting to feel a bit rough and I feel pretty dirty. The clothes I'm wearing have the wear and grime from the days before. I'm looking forward to a wash! Haven't managed a snow shower yet but I think I might have to at some point soon. My face is browned from the constant powerful sun and my eyes are white from the shades. I look like an Arctic explorer, but then again I am one now.

Dad wrote a short journal during his time with the expedition. This midway point seems a natural break, so we dropped it in here. Then you can pick up my diary again, to the end.

Firstly I'll give you a quick idea of his involvement. A few months before the expedition, Will contacted my dad to see if he would like to join the trip, and if not for the whole trip then part of it. With Dad's passion and focus on the issue of global warming, it would be a perfect opportunity for him to see first hand the effects it is having on the arctic. By joining he would help create awareness about the problems they are having up in the snowy world on top of our planet. I was asked by Will to reach a younger audience and help capture the interest of my peer group.

Richard's Diary: Dad Writes

Two places I had never been are the Arctic and the Antarctic. I have always been fascinated by the idea of the Antarctic, ever since I learned as a child that my grandfather's cousin was Scott of the Antarctic - the famous explorer. When my class learned about him at school, I felt very proud.

Robert Falcon Scott was a British sea captain and led two expeditions to the South Pole. He died in 1912 on the disastrous second trip, along with his crew. I was also interested by the fact that he had crossed the Antarctic in a balloon - which perhaps sparked my own great interest in ballooning. Later, I came to know his son, Peter, well, and through him gained my lifelong interest in nature conservation.

So when Diane Isaacs of Green Mountain Productions - she's president of the film company owned by Melanie Griffith and Antonio Banderas - approached me to get involved with a film she was producing about global warming in the Arctic and the effects of it on the Inuit people, I jumped in with both feet. Or should that be, dived in headfirst? Diane linked me up with Will Steger, who was heading up the Baffin Island expedition. When I realised that the entire expedition would be over fifteen hundred miles, over four months, I knew my other commitments wouldn't allow it.

I asked Will to describe the various sections of the expedition and, in the end, decided to join on the last leg of the trip from Clyde River to Iglulik. I was told that this section afforded dramatic mountainous scenery, which later turned into the traditional flat Arctic landscape. We would live amongst the Inuit - albeit briefly - in two 'almost' traditional coastal settlements, cross Baffin Island with dog teams and a few outfitters (hunters) and see a good cross section of the land on the way. Most importantly, I would hear and see for myself how climate change was affecting their lives. It was lovely, too, to be travelling with my son, Sam.

I had intended to do tons of training for the trip, but an accident with a quad bike in Spain damaged my arm and shoulder and I had to take it easy, with some gentle exercise. On top of that, my plans for launching new airlines in Nigeria and Kenya and developing a wonderful new game reserve on Masai Mara land (not to mention an elephants' highway across country to Mount Kenya!) meant I had spent several weeks in the heat of Africa. Not the best way to train for a challenging journey across the Arctic in sub zero temperatures.

Read on . . .

A tarpaulin was laid out in the middle of the village hall. Three frozen stag heads, cut off from their frozen bodies that lay next to them, stared out at us. Chunks of raw frozen meat cut from one of the stags lay there awaiting us. Large frozen fish lay next to them. This was the feast the Inuit had laid on for us at Clyde River to help us on our way.

Inuit kids running happily around to each of us – 'Are you the millionaire! Are you the billionaire!' Speeches from the elders urging us to go to Congress to allow them to still earn money by taking Americans to kill the occasional polar bear. Strange, since one of the reasons we were here was to alert the world to how it should save the polar bear. When I stood up and mentioned my son Sam was on the trip loud clapping broke out from around the room. The Inuit are very close to their families. Sam, my 21-year-old son, had come to Clyde River to join Will Steger's 1,200-mile Global Warming 101 Expedition to help alert the world to what global warming was doing to the Arctic and the Inuit, and what in turn that could do to the rest of the world. Sam planned to travel with them skiing behind husky dogs from Clyde River to Iglulik. They kindly offered to have me too for part of their trip.

Having somehow managed to avoid offending by not tucking into the frozen meat and fish (and choosing the kids' cakes instead) we headed home for an early night, sober, since the Inuit community has banned alcohol due to problems with it in the past years.

The husky dogs were raring to go early the next morning. Howling, pulling at their ropes, desperate to be on the move. The kids had been given the morning off school so the sleds were piled high with them. 'Can we come? Please!?' Hundreds of innocent questions. The sleds had also been piled high with tents, sleeping bags, seals for dog food, clothes.

Sam had already been training for a week, learning how to run the dogs, to ski behind the sled. He looked so comfortable. So comfortable, in fact, I wasn't sure I'd get him home. He had always felt more at home with the local people in the Caribbean than the expats, having been brought up there. Now he felt completely at home with the Inuit.

Simon was in charge of my sled. Theo was my guide. I went off to find some water only to turn around to find the dogs hadn't been able to wait any longer. The sled had headed off down the valley with Theo and Simon running after it. I set off in hot pursuit.

Finally we were off. Sam was alongside with a huge smile on his face. Skis on, holding onto the back of the sled. His first big personal adventure.

Simon had bought two new five-month-old puppy huskies at Clyde River to supplement his ten-strong team. It soon became apparent that they were slower than the other dogs and couldn't keep up. I didn't enjoy the first few hours because of this, but I realised it was part of their training. The other ten dogs seemed to love Simon and they presumably had gone through the same thing.

Suddenly we headed down from Clyde Fjord – a glaciated valley flooded by sea water. It was quite awesome. Certainly one of the wonders of the world. Our tiny sleds in the middle of this great fjord. This wonderful wilderness.

Travelling at six miles per hour we covered thirty miles in five hours and then set up camp as the sun dimmed to the sounds of howling dogs (it would be light all night since at this time of year they have virtually 24-hour daylight). We went off in search of the perfect ice for drinking water and tea and broke it with an axe.

Awake most of the first night with dogs barking, dogs howling (at one moment, howling hysterically). I assumed a polar bear had entered the camp. If they weren't howling or barking I could hear them all night long chewing on ice or chewing bones right outside the tent. When I did drift off I would awake to frozen icicles in my hair, on my face, my neck and my jacket that I used as a pillow. Altogether an interesting first night – I wonder how Sam had slept?

The two young pups had cried the whole of the first night, setting off the rest of the packs. Our tents had been placed in the middle of the dogs to protect us from the polar bears. After that night I'd rather sleep with the bears!

I was sharing the tent with Will Steger, the leader of the expedition. He'd spent most of his life on the ice having gone to both North and South Poles and having come very close to losing his life on a number of occasions.

Interestingly one of his heroes was Scott of the Antarctic, whose life had also inspired me as a youngster to become an adventurer. It looked like Sam had caught the same bug.

The next day, tired and cold, but yet another gorgeous day. Thawed ice in the large kettle to make tea. Struggled to put on Arctic clothes in tent.

Headed off into the most spectacular scenery. Towering mountains as we travelled down the fjord in the middle of the ice. Melting glaciers – dramatically towering over the fjord. Neck getting sore looking at vast mountains and scenery.

After half an hour of trying to encourage his two new pups to keep up, Simon finally stopped the sled and cut them loose. The puppies slouched off and followed slowly behind the sled.

Our sled from being last now surged ahead. We travelled thirty miles. The most beautiful thirty miles I'd ever travelled. The scenery was quite literally awesome. A national and international treasure.

As it was getting dark a speck appeared in the distance behind us, gradually getting closer. Was it a bear? A seal? An arctic fox? Then suddenly we saw it was the pups. Simon smiled at me knowingly. He looked pleased to see them. The pups had proven they were the fittest and in the frozen north the survival of the fittest is taken quite literally. They were hooked up to the dogs at the front of the sled and made sure they never slipped again. I had a feeling they would become the strongest and most loyal husky dogs they had.

That night we touched down on the edge of the fjord. On a glacier valley overlooking more spectacular scenery we learned how to get our tents up very quickly so as to prepare for the Arctic storm conditions ahead, how to shovel ice around the edges of the tent to stop being blown away, how to find the best ice for drinking water, the best ice to hide behind when going for a very cold – what's the word? – shit.

Sam had joined us in the tent to share what he'd learned so far about global warming that we could take to the outside world. He'd also smuggled in a very welcome flask of sloe gin from England, which we rationed out.

Climbed into sleeping bags. Put two pairs of underpants over my head to avoid the frost of the night before.

Next day we finished travelling down the fjord and came out into the most heart-stirring ice world imaginable. A massive frozen river of magnificent colours of blue. Stunning – the real swan lake.

We crossed it with dogs sliding in every direction. Our pup just couldn't stand on his feet and dragged behind the sled. But this time Simon didn't cut him loose. He'd learned about the sensitivities of us Southerners. Then off the river onto a narrow ravine and a long climb over the mountains. Again a stunning ravine, which was overlooked by natural ice sculptures. Even our guides said they'd seen nothing like it.

But it was hot and the dogs struggled up it in the melting snow. We too were exhausted, running alongside the dogs.

By the end of the trip I'll be very fit; running alongside the sled when the dogs are struggling, jumping on when they speed up, running again when they slow up and so on all day.

The next day up the highest part of the mountain – really hard work. My body really feeling it. My arm aching, having turned that quad bike over six weeks before. My legs in agony from sheer overuse. Was I finally showing my age or lack of fitness! Glad to hear Sam felt exhausted too.

What goes up has to come down. That is when sledding with dogs is most dangerous. Most sled drivers put on 'binders' to slow up their sleds as they go down a hill. Simon just goes for it. I didn't remain standing on the back of the sled for long. As we turned the first corner out of control I was thrown onto the rocks. I watched Simon careering on down the hill as pots and pans, sleeping bags and tents spewed across the country-side. The dogs, not wishing to be run over by the heavy sled, just went faster and faster. Somehow Simon clung on.

Coming out of the mountains we started travelling across miles of Arctic waste. This was what I'd imagined the Arctic to be like. Not the magnificent scenery of the last few days. For miles we travelled through similar bleak-looking country. Then, suddenly, ahead in the distance we saw the most magnificent cliffs. Even more magnificent than the White Cliffs of Dover, but just as white and bright. We'd come across the Barnes Ice Cap.

Ice that had been there since the last Ice Age, 10,000 years ago, and perhaps before. 75 miles long, 30 miles wide and 3,000 feet deep. Once again, stunning colours. And yet in the last ten years it had begun to melt.

Theo, my guide, told me how they used to be able to see the top of it from the Foxe Basin – where the expedition is heading for – dominating the horizon. Sadly, no longer. The same was happening to the glaciers. All of us could now clearly see the blue ice melting. If it continues this picturesque land of rock, ice and snow could one day just become rock. As a result of the thawing glaciers the rivers were now flowing quicker and causing some to create new courses. More water in the short term but – the Inuit are bright enough to know – less water in the long term.

Theo also pointed out other disturbing signs. As the sea is getting warmer the killer whales are moving north in ever increasing numbers. The eider ducks and phalaropes are now staying north all year round instead of just the summer. Even in the dark of winter when there's just two hours of sunlight they stay. The ground squirrel that used to be found 250 miles south of his village of Iglulik is now flourishing around there. They are getting new species of birds. The hoary redpoll, a small song-bird, has found its way up north. The greenfinch showed up for the first time at Theo's window ledge this winter. The waxwing – that is normally found in the marshes and trees further south rather than the Arctic north – is now appearing there. Even the robin has arrived for the first time.

The squid and octopus that never before showed up in the food chain are now becoming commonplace. 'When we first heard about glo-bal warming we Inuit thought it was good news. Our kids would have warmer winters. Now we know it's not good news. It is changing the eco-system altogether. This beautiful world we live in is going to disappear.'

Crossing another fjord, a ringed seal sticks his head out of a breath-ing hole. They keep them open through constant use. The ice used to be six-foot thick here. Now it's three-foot thick. This year Theo has lost three friends through the ice due to the unpredictability of it. The ringed seal can stay under for twenty minutes – some stay longer when being hunted. The ringed seal grows to about three feet long. There's a healthy number of ringed seal in Greenland, Alaska, Siberia and Canada. The Inuit use them for food for themselves and their dogs, for heating for their igloos and shelters, for clothing. 'They are our cow,' says Theo, 'but their economic value is being killed off by animal activists from the West.' (Greenpeace is hated by the Inuit.) The Inuit live off the land like we do but where their food is seal, ours is cattle.

Having said that, Theo attacked the wanton killing of seals in Greenland where they cull the numbers simply to protect the fish population. He believes there's enough fish without having to do that. The seals used to just have the bears and humans as their principal predators. However, because of global warming there are now fewer lemmings. The snow melting then freezing makes it more difficult for lemmings to get to their food just under the hard crust surface of the snow. The soft snow, of exactly the right texture, helped them create long runs, and insulated them from extreme cold. Lack of a thick snow cover has resulted in the arctic fox and wolf, that used to live off the lemmings, adding seals to their diet. Likewise, the snowy owl has moved on because of the shortage of lemmings.

Another seal hole, on a tidal crack in the ice. The seals like these cracks because the ice is thinner so they can keep their breathing holes open for longer. The polar bears like to be where the ice is rough, because there, it creates snow banks. That is where the seals make their dens for their young and where they love to laze around. We saw our first polar bear jumping into such a den to eat the young seals.

Another group of Inuit who dislike Greenpeace live in the Foxe Basin, where there's a large quantity of walrus that they live off – as the

Masai live off their cattle, and American ranchers and Welsh farmers live off their livestock. It enables the Inuit to have time to learn music, visit relatives, have large, close-knit families and not just survive on subsistence living.

Having spent my time with these strong, remarkable people I have complete sympathy with them on their fight to awaken the world to global warming and what it's going to do to their community. I sympathise completely on their right to live off the seal and walrus. But I believe they are making a large mistake in allowing hunters to come and kill their polar bears. Polar bears should be their tigers, their leopards, their elephants. A majestic animal to attract tourists to come and marvel at. To earn a quick buck here will kill off their heritage for the future.

Sleeping in Sam's tent the last night. It has been wonderful to join him and Will's trip across the Arctic.

My last night was particularly cold. We all have a piss bottle in our beds due to it being too cold to get out in the night. Well – I didn't do the top of the bottle up tightly enough. Woke up to find my sleeping bag consisted of frozen piss. I told the story the next day and everyone had a good laugh at my expense!

Tuesday 1 May: the last morning. Bizarrely had to leave to announce our American airline Virgin America as the Department of Transport brought the announcement forward. Strange having been on a trip alerting people to the perils of global warming, then leaving early to announce a new airline. However, at least all Virgin's profits from it are going to develop clean fuels, unlike our rival airlines. We are hoping that in January 2008 we will fly the first engine of one of our 747s on clean fuels. So a lot of these resources are being well spent. Hopefully it won't be too long for people to fly again without guilt.

Otto bravely carried on filming without goggles in order to get the best shots. Very dangerous, however. Fortunately we covered up his eyes in time so no permanent damage was done. Because of my arm injury I was unable to ski or learn to run the dogs, so couldn't contribute a lot to the expedition personally apart from bringing attention to it. Sam was very fit and it soon became apparent that Dad should hand over to son, who was far better equipped than he. It was also clear to me very quickly that this was Sam's adventure, not mine, and that he'd return for more – next year, Greenland.

I waved Sam and Will goodbye as they headed off into a snowstorm. It has been an honour and privilege to share this adventure with them, their quest to alert the world to global warming. They were now carrying on, whilst a Twin Otter landed on the ice to take me off to a bath and warm bed.

I'm flying out with my wonderful nephew Otto. Watching the plane land made your stomach turn. With all the rocks and snow drifts to avoid, they must be brave pilots!

Finally: Why should we be concerned about what happens in the Arctic? Why should we care about the small signals here and there that we picked up on this trip? Well, apart from protecting the Inuit and the beauty of their land, what happens to them will come back and bite us with a vengeance.

Much of their land has been permanently frozen, with something called permafrost. If that permanently frozen land warms up it will release enough methane to raise the temperature of the world by

2.5 degrees - resulting in a catastrophe. So their world and ours are inextricably linked. We have to take note and do something.

You'd think the Inuit would be resentful about what we are doing to their world. But they are such mellow people. 'We'll adapt,' they say. 'Will you adapt?'

We flew over Sam on the way home, Iglulik the first stop. Saw him waving. Saw all of them mooning us! His sled had gone through the ice and his and Will's sleeping bags were soaked. Not sure what they'll do tonight. Somehow they'll manage.

We're going to attempt to turn this trip into a film about global warming and the Inuit. Hopefully something good will come of it. I certainly didn't follow in the footsteps of my relative Scott of the Antarctic, but I got a glimpse of what he'd been through. I just hope Sam gets no more than a glimpse these next two weeks.

Sam should be in charge of his own dogsled from today. Proud dad.

The Rest of My Diary

... continued from after Dad left.

Wednesday 2 May
35 miles

Today for me was the toughest day yet. It could have been a combination of different things. Dad and Otto leaving, missing my girlfriend, the change in weather, riding on Simon's sled where sitting can become quite monotonous and cold (and conversation doesn't last longer than ten seconds at a time), or just being worn out. I had a restful day and the views were spectacular but I couldn't seem to shrug off the slight down feeling. Sitting on the sled instead of skiing – you get pretty cold.

The weather turned much cooler today, quite brisk, with cloudy skies, slight snowfall and a small breeze. We had a low kind of ice fog this morning – the first time since we left Clyde River – so that I couldn't see the other sleds travelling with us. It's more comfortable not to be in the direct line of fire from the sun's rays and all that damaging ultraviolet light and the dogs are happier when it's cooler. The sun has been brutal here for the past week.

After continuing down the northern headwaters of the MacDonald, we came to a section of frozen rapids in some small canyons and had to aggressively steer the sled in between the rocks. Lying on the sled I drifted in and out of sleep and awoke each time to a bump on a rock or a sharp change in direction. Will also rode while Lukie mushed – and as he said later, it was hard for him to sit still – usually he likes to ski or run. Will is a geologist, which is interesting, especially when he describes what we're seeing. Canyons give a good slice of geology. The geology of this area is igneous and metamorphic hard-rock types. As we descend through the canyons we can see the various layers. We followed the full length of the MacDonald River. Then the river widened out quite a bit and we entered Lake Gillian. It is a huge frozen lake, miles long in different directions, surrounded by mountains. Riding the last stretch was quite a treat. The moody sky with silver shards peered through the clouds as the sun's rays tried to hit the ground, creating pools of white liquid on the snow. A sled was off into the distance and what a sight, small against that vast expanse and seeming to float in a radiant light.

After travelling for eleven hours straight plus a one-hour break for lunch, we finally came to camp. We made a lot of ground today (35 miles, travelling from 5.30 a.m. to 7.30 p.m.) and are a little ahead of schedule; we might take the morning off tomorrow, if not the whole day. I'm looking forward to my first lie-in and am ready for a much-needed rest. 'What doesn't kill you makes you stronger.'

I'm tenting with Will and while he tidied up a little, I put together a caribou and rice dinner. We're switching tent partners tomorrow. I'll go in with Stetson and Will with Theo. Will gets on really well with Theo – who he has said is one of the best teachers he's had in life. He met him three years ago, when passing through his traditional village on a 2,000-mile dog-team expedition. He recognised him as a very special person and recruited him for this expedition we're now on. Will says his knowledge on wildlife, land and Inuit culture is encyclopaedic. We learn a great deal from him – stuff that older people remember is vital for future generations, especially when their culture has changed. We've had some great adventures. You never know what's going to happen day to day; there are always new things to see. We discussed how Will had always wanted to see the Barnes Ice Cap, for example – and we ended up being close to it for four or five days. When we were up there we saw ravens, and a gyre falcon came out of its nest and flew over the dogs. There were also a lot of snow buntings. I wonder what they feed on in that wilderness of barren rocks and bare ice?

Thursday 3 May

As the dogs run, the snow compacts under their feet and, somehow, it forms little icy balls between their pads, which press on tender areas and obviously hurt. Every now and then as we go along, I notice the dogs trying to bite their feet – not easy to do without stopping. The Inuit guys make the dogs keep going, but if it looks bad, Stetson will stop. He's even got little blue booties for his favourites, Whisper and Jones, both lead dogs. Whisper is the best trained of the lot, a great dog. Stopping constantly slows us right down and with the early spring and the sea ice starting to melt, it's important to keep going. But we made such good ground yesterday and are ahead of schedule we decided to take a couple of days off. Letting the dogs rest and heal their cut feet will make travelling in the thick snow much better.

What a lovely day. It was overcast, which can make it relatively warm. A light sun day, though some blue. We're close to the ocean, albeit a frozen bay – but there are some open-water areas, especially in the middle, so blue sky apparently is typical for open water. There was a little light snow on the ground. The dogs, all stretched out, looked content.

I think yesterday was so tough as it was just so long and tiring. We've done three hundred miles in eight days' hard travel and we're still coming down off rocky hills. In two days, we will be on Foxe Basin, the northern extension of Hudson Bay – then we'll be on sea ice and a bit of land. But travel conditions should be good.

It is great to have some chill time. It's been pretty hard to take it all in as so far it's been nonstop: travelling all day and then setting up camp, cooking dinner and sorting equipment before much-needed sleep.

A daily routine generally consists of

- Wake up at 6 a.m., melt ice
- Eat breakfast
- Pack up equipment and stove
- Pack up tent and ice screws
- Load up sleds
- Harness dogs – tie them up
- Travel – one hour lunch break
- Finish around 7 p.m.
- Unpack sleds
- Unharness dogs, tie them to ice screws
- Set up camp
- Find/axe ice and melt for cooking water
- Cook dinner
- Write in diary
- Sleep

I'm glad to have the day to reflect and take in the surroundings. How self-confident I feel. In a way it's good that the others have gone, as I am here to look after myself. I have no close friends or Dad to rely on. While it's been amazing to share this experience with my dad, I feel now it's time that I make my own way. I feel like I have grown a lot doing this and have learned so much. Although I'm social and enjoy the company of friends and family, I'm also quite introspective, and love periods of solitude wherever I am in the world. I think a lot and dream, write songs, and let my imagination soar. A place like this - a frozen lake in the arms of misty mountains and hills - is almost like the setting of *Swan Lake*. It's lyrically romantic, beautiful, yet harsh. The colours are incredible - not bright colours, but the muted shades that Camille Pissarro might use in his snow scenes; white and grey, with subtle undertones of pink and pistachio green, dusky blue and lilac. You can see colour in anything when you look. Then mist comes down and everything is blotted out. I could be floating anywhere in this invisible landscape, alone in my dreams and imagination. There's no sound - absolutely nothing - then someone moves, or ice cracks, snow shifts and whispers to you, the dogs chatter and yawn in their deep, curled up sleep. At feeding time you can hear them chew on chunks of frozen seal and their leads rattle; they growl, they snap. I think of the world under the snow and ice - the bears in their dens, the seals out on the ice, lemmings scampering in their invisible runs, fish swimming strongly against the currents.

Tent life is enjoyable. I love the simplicity of it. Tenting with Will is good; we both have our own space and also chat about different things, like his struggles with the life he leads. Funny thing he told me is that he had got to like using a pee bottle on his trips and takes one everywhere he goes, even to hotels. He says that the women he's with don't like it very much. No wonder!

Due to the weather everyone stayed in their own tents. It's been quite nice to be alone with the environment. A peaceful, relaxing day to reflect and take in the quietness from the expanse of space around me. Cheesy pasta for dinner and some more of my book, *Northern Lights* by Philip Pullman.

Keeping the temperature right inside your tent is a skill. We have 81°F in our tent, without heat on. I didn't realise how important colours are when choosing a tent. They can affect mood and – as now – temperature. So, according to Will, who was happy to explain all the little tricks he had learned, the rule of thumb seems to be, cooler colours – greens – for hot places and warm colours (not red) for cold. Here's a summary from Will – for campers, it might prove pretty handy to know this stuff.

Picking the right colour for your tent is really important for two things: mood and heat absorption. Our tent is olive drab canvas, yellow inside, which gives a good light. Even when the sun is behind clouds (as now) this colour absorbs a lot of energy, which makes for a very warm and comfortable environment. Our tent is dry inside for the first time this expedition. We have experimented with colour over the years on many expeditions. The colour you don't want is blue (or green) on an ice cap. We did it once, and regretted it. It sets a real moody tone. We had a kind of red once – not good. The best colour is olive drab. It's sort of a handy colour, between orange and yellow – maybe with a yellow fly – which is good for gathering energy. This colour also casts a very good mood. But you can also overheat — so it depends on where you are. You wouldn't really want yellow or red in the Sahara Desert. We have learned one trick though. During 24-hour sunlight, or if you're in a hot place with constant sun (with whatever colour tent), throw black tarps over your tent to try to get shade and to relax a bit more in a darker situation.

Friday 4 May

It's rare to have two days off like this. We are down to eight people now and felt a kind of comradeship, and yet isolation. It's so quiet out here. The world seems very far away – and yet, with all that's going on in terms of the climate, we are inextricably linked to everyone. It's as if the Arctic is the start of a universal train and when it moves, the rest of the world is attached and has to follow. Some people might call it a 'knock-on effect'. I think, now that we're nearing the end of the expedition and have this time to reflect, everyone is cocooned in their cosy tents, pondering what we have achieved by making this effort – and will achieve, when we get back into the world.

Stetson is a very positive, fun-loving kind of guy; yet he has his private pain, that somehow is linked to the environment. He can be serious at times when we talk. Today, he has been thinking about what this expedition means. He and the others have spent several months trying to do their part to help change things. We pollute even the air that we breathe. This is very real to him because of his wife Shelly's cancer. She has been battling it for several years and despite everything, she has faith that we can solve atmosphere and carbon pollutions.

Ed says, 'Everyone has to do their part.' The Inuit are a fun-loving people, but they – probably more than most – take global warming seriously. They are committed to spreading the word because it directly affects them. Their lives can depend on it. But it's more than global warming. When even the food you eat is laced with heavy poisons, carried in the Arctic food chain, from fish to seals to whales, due to uncontrolled industrial run off thousands of miles away, it's crucial to be aware of everything around you.

Many other things are changing too, such as the strength and the direction of the wind. Wind, a defining characteristic of the Arctic environment, is a navigational tool. Snow formations caused by strong winds have acted as reliable landmarks for generations, but the direction of the wind has shifted in the past five years and is often quite fickle. Inuit hunters and travellers often find themselves lost in their own back yard. When we feel the wind against our faces, we snug our hoods down tighter and move forward across the snowy landscape – but the Inuit who loses his bearings can lose his life.

By the end of the day, everyone had written a ton of deep as well as poetical thoughts. It seems that being almost alone in the Arctic taps a deep well of inspiration and contemplation. I thought this entry from Elizabeth's journal was interesting enough to share with you. She mentions that there are many Inuit words for snow. I've included a few at the end, in 'The Heavy Stuff'.

Snowy rest day

On and off through the day it snowed. I enjoyed watching the quality of the snowflakes change over the course of the day. When it was warm and very calm, the flakes were large and fluffy, almost like the white cottony seeds that blow from a dandelion. When the weather warmed up a bit and the wind began to blow, the snow fell in heavier sleety drops that were almost rain and melted as soon as they hit our jackets and tent rainflies. I remembered back to earlier in the expedition when it was colder and the flakes were much smaller and with a less intricate crystal-line structure.

I have often heard it said that Inuit people have hundreds of Inuktitut words for snow. I have asked many Inuit people if this is true and some will laugh and say, 'Perhaps not hundreds ... but very, very many.' One thing is certain — slight changes in the wind, humidity and temperature can produce very different kinds of snow.

Now that the climate is warming in the Arctic, there are more incidents of freezing rain and thaw-freeze events. These can coat the vegetation with a layer of ice that can make it difficult for caribou to reach food. These events can also disrupt the habitat of under-snow dwellers like voles and lemmings. Rains can also collapse polar bear dens.

For us today, any snow is welcome snow. We have miles to travel before we reach the sea ice. The diminishing snow cover is exposing rocks, gravel and sand which makes travel difficult and wears out the sled runners. We are hoping that the snow continues through the night and covers some of the rocks to make our travel easier tomorrow.

Elizabeth

Saturday 5 May
33 miles

A long, hard day today. We're 15 miles off Foxe Station, 150 miles north of the Arctic Circle and heading for Grant-Suttie Bay. We'll be off the MacDonald river system and on sea ice tomorrow – or as Ed says, 'From source to sea'. It's a bit confusing – to someone like me, who's never done this before – because it seems we can be on the sea, yet also still on a frozen lake and a frozen river. Ed explained the schedule: 'We will spend the next five days working our way towards Iglulik. The first days we will be travelling on frozen Link Lake and then Link River. After about two days, we should then be on the frozen sea ice of the Foxe Basin. We will spend the following three days skirting the coastline of Baffin Island as we work our way northward and westward towards Iglulik.'

But this makes sense. Strong ocean currents flow through parts of the Foxe Basin, keeping the ice from freezing solidly like it does in some other areas. For this reason people who travel between Iglulik and Clyde River, instead of travelling in a straight line across the Foxe Basin, hug the coastline and cut over land in some areas to avoid open water. In the past the ice in Foxe Basin would go out near the end of July or beginning of August – but now the ice goes out at the end of June or beginning of July. According to the Canadian Ice Service map dated 26 February there was thick ice across Foxe Basin. By 12 March, however, the ice along the edge of Foxe Basin near Iglulik had started to thin. By 9 April, the area of thin ice had increased by around 600 per cent. Even though we will be skirting the edge of the Foxe Basin and cutting over the land to avoid open water and poor ice, it is difficult for us not to feel a tiny bit of apprehension about the thinning ice on our route ahead.

After waking at about 5.30 a.m. with a good rest in me we got up and headed straight off. There was a top layer of snow added over yesterday and during the night so travel was slow and tough. I was riding with Stetson today, which made a pleasant change in conversation from Simon's sled (i.e. there was some!).

It's fun being around Stetson. He got onto the subject of socks. I didn't really know if he was joking when he announced that he had changed his socks for the first time on the trip. 'I have a spare pair but was saving them. Now that we're on the last leg I thought I would swap. It feels so good. I still haven't changed my ice-warmer underwear. Guess I'll wear it all the way into Iglulik. It looks as good as new.' But he did have a twinkle in his voice. Like when he was tenting with Ed and mentioned that he was reading Ed's book (*No Shortcuts to the Top*) but pretended that he had forgotten the title. He said they'd be able to swap stories – Ed about climbing Everest and K2 and 'his nemesis' Annapurna – while Stetson could describe climbing the hill in his back yard.

We pushed through the thick snow in a northwesterly direction, with only two small breaks and the terrain gradually got flatter. I think today has been my toughest physically. My legs are almost dead after more than ten hours pretty much nonstop in thick snow. You feel it.

As we headed off the land down a big sloping hillside, we came onto a large lake – apparently, the start of sea ice. It's fun manoeuvring around the rocks at some speed, apart from the dogs bolting and fighting. It was the burst of adrenaline I wanted. The days are becoming a mental game of clocking up the miles and grinding down the legs.

After some ten and a half hours of straight travel, we arrived on the sea ice at a place called the Bay of the Ocean. It's a beautiful spot and we've started on the home straight. It's taken us nine days to traverse Baffin Island – tough on us and the dogs. In the five days we have left to reach our journey's end, we'll have to clock around thirty miles per day. We have further to travel because of the unusual weather conditions, which in turn have started to melt the ice we'd normally be travelling over.

The higher Arctic warms up faster with the return of the plankton to the Atlantic in the spring – this in turn makes the sea ice off the north-eastern side of Baffin Island warmer and the weather more unsettled. The area south-west of Baffin Island is usually one of the coldest areas of the Arctic – and Iglulik is usually the coldest place. It is known as a stronghold of the cold. According to Will, when he passed through this area three years ago on a 2,000-mile trip, six inches of soft snow settled on wind-pack surfaces in May, making for ideal travel conditions. It's similar now – but ten degrees warmer. This meant there were more open places on the sea ice, and the ice was thinner; the weather was also unsettled. At the moment, with it being relatively mild, we're enjoying the spring weather. However, normally we would have just cut across the Foxe Basin on frozen sea ice to reach Iglulik, as hunters have always done. It would have got us there a lot faster. But since there's now open water out there, we need to hug the west coastline of Baffin, head north and then veer towards the west. Then we'll kind of arc up around the coastline of Baffin and several islands and then head south again, to Iglulik.

We're camped for the night by open water, and because of this there's a thick fog; a pretty normal cycle here. We had very strong heat yesterday at four or five in the afternoon, and this makes the fog. It's great for us because it keeps the ultraviolet light down. It's a dangerous time of year for UV because of the ozone hole. We really did feel it all day yesterday – so today, we felt very fortunate to have a cool windy day with a little bit of snow from the ocean. It's perfect for running the dogs.

Sleeping out here on the sea ice is a little dangerous as it's polar bear country so we have to be ultra alert and I keep my knife by my bed, just in case. I just made a quick call on the sat phone to a mate who's having a night out with the boys. What a contrast. Clubbing with your friends has its ups, but right now I'd rather be here!

Sunday 6 May
35 miles

Riding on Simon's sled today was chilled. We woke up and headed off over the frozen sea. Travelling here is consistent with the flat ice, but the snow is pretty thick and you have to plough on through. I brought my book along today, which was a treat as it broke up the day well. I was absorbed between the two different worlds of the Arctic: one, *Northern Lights*, a fantasy tale of witches and armoured bears, and the other, real polar bears and the elements around.

The sky was open and the sun was shining bright, casting its rays upon all it touched, and everything it did land on seemed to shine intensely. We're all suffering from sunburn – the dangerous kind you get from ultraviolet rays. We all have our own methods of dealing with it and protecting ourselves. Elizabeth has been making a study of it. She says there can be no fashion consciousness when your skin is burning. Ever since we left Clyde River the sun has been relentless. It rises well before we wake and doesn't set until we are fast asleep. It reflects off all the white snow and ice and burns even the undersides of our noses and under our chins. Stetson, Abby and Elizabeth slather on the zinc oxide sunblock and don baseball caps and bandannas. We joke that with the thick white paste on our faces we look a bit like geishas or clowns. One day, when Elizabeth's zinc layer was especially thick, Stetson asked if she was trying to scare away the polar bears. Will covers up with his hood and a leather 'beak' that attaches to the bridge of his sunglasses and covers his nose and cheeks. The famous mountaineer Reinhold Messner gave the beak to Will when they were both preparing for expeditions in Antarctica in 1990. Ed's preferred method for beating the sun is to wear a baseball cap, glacier glasses and a hood. It's difficult to stay cool enough with a hood up, however, when the sun is warm and you're exercising.

It's not just the snow and the 24-hour daylight that makes us vulnerable here in the Arctic. The thinned ozone layer lets through more UV radiation than you would get further south. Although many people confuse the two issues, global warming and the ozone hole are separate issues. Stratospheric ozone thinning was caused by chlorofluorocarbons that are now banned, and the ozone layer is beginning to repair itself. Here in the Arctic, however, the ozone layer is slower to recover. This is due in part to the effect of global warming on stratospheric temperatures. During the spring the ozone layer is at its thinnest so we, along with the other living things in the Arctic, are exposed to the greatest amount of UV radiation. For plants and animals, spring is also the time in their life cycles where they are most vulnerable to damage from UV radiation.

After another long flat stretch (the second longest so far – 35 miles) we came to camp on a tiny island made of sedimentary rocks, just a few feet above sea level. Will, ever the geologist, pointed out some brachio-pod fossils. These tiny little shells – also known as lampshells – still exist today, but are almost extinct, having gradually declined over the past hundred million years. Mind-blowing!

As we rode into camp the others saw some polar bear tracks, a mother and two cubs. They had tried to break a seal den but there were no seals there. Producer/cameraman Jerry Stenger saw two more bears today near here, so the dogs are positioned around us and I have a spade by my bag. I don't know what it could do but it might help me sleep better.

The sun – the largest I've seen – still shining bright, is blanketing a warm glow over the dogs' coats. At camp there was an inukshuk nearby and peaks of ice flowing off into the horizon. During the day Inuit outfit-ters shot and skinned a wolf. They left the skinned body and took the head and skin to sell. They will only get 170 dollars for it. What a sight; the huge, bloody body intact and gruesome, but no skin. This is certainly another way of life.

Walking around I felt the ground move and clumps of ice all around me chased each other. What a fright, but the others reassured me that it is pretty safe here and the only thing to worry about is polar bears. (*Reassured* me?) Stetson is tenting with Will. He told him that he's very willing to give him some Arctic tips, which he was sure Will would be very keen to listen to. Tomorrow Ed and I are going to solo mush, bor-rowing Abby's sled. Stetson said dryly that should we survive, we'll go on to the end, driving a dog team together. Better get some rest! Going to need it.

Monday 7 May
34 miles

Last night, I awoke in a daze with the sounds of the dogs blaring and voices. Through the commotion I heard someone shout, 'Polar bear!' With those words I immediately felt a chill come over my body. A hundred thoughts raced through my mind. How close was it? Was someone hurt? I looked at my watch, which read 2.30 a.m. Oh shit. I jumped out of my sleeping bag, Ed was already out the door. When I came out I saw the bear was close, but not so close that we didn't have time to act. It was about fifty feet away, and surrounded by the morning mist, making it seem somewhat mysterious. The low lying sun coated its white fur in a yellowish light, and its breath condensed in the cold air. I rushed back in and grabbed my camera. Everyone was out of their tents in their underwear. Stetson had his boxers on, a beanie and a shotgun! The bear stared us down, then started to run towards us. John fired a cracker shell into the air. These are projectiles like firework bangers that go off loudly and are very good for scaring bears away. The bear was a little startled and stopped its charge, but didn't retreat.

The bear was magnificent. It was the size of a truck but as agile as a cat. We could see it smelling the air and checking us out as it walked closer. When it got to about thirty feet away one of the Inuit guys (Lukie's brother-in-law) shot another cracker shell in the air. There are two cracker shells in the gun intended to frighten the bear, but they have enough power to kill a person. The rest of the slugs are live ammo. After this shot was fired the bear startled but charged forward again with real purpose. It looked hungry. It was a large male bear and they don't scare easily. After a moment of thought he ran towards the tents again. At this point Stetson shouted, 'Get him out of here!' He could tell the bear was ready to attack and was showing all the signs of dangerous behaviour. He fired some shots in the air and so did Lukie's brother-in-law. The bear luckily moved back a little, still eyeing up his targets.

The Inuit are polar bear hunters by culture and one of them now ran towards the bear firing live shots just by it. The bear ran away and gradually melted into the snow around him. Wow, what a feeling! Scared, exhilarated, awed, what an impressive creature. It moved with such grace and power but, however harmless it could seem, you could tell it was a stealth bomber – sleek and beautiful but deadly.

The sky was clearing and the sun only sinks below the horizon for about an hour now. The light in the sky remains bright 24 hours. So we could see the bear in his full glory. What a great memory. I kept thinking, what if he'd managed to get in? What if we didn't wake up?

Despite the cold, we all stood around talking about it for a moment or two. Everyone except Stetson had now emerged from their tents fully dressed. Stetson said the bear was friendly – he just wanted to join us. Must have done, since he ran into camp. That's one way of looking at it. Will's opinion was that the bear was very brave, coming into an Inuit camp. We had three hunters with us, and the film crew had three more. One bear and six experienced hunters – no contest really when guns are involved.

Trying to sleep after that wasn't easy. The dogs were on edge and they made a lot of noise. Trying to distinguish between their alarm call and playful fighting is not easy. On the one hand you try to shut the noise out. On the other hand the noise is the only sound to alarm you if a polar bear is coming. It could mean the difference between life and death, and you need to be alert. I woke up a few times in the night but there were no more problems. I feel a lot safer knowing the Inuit guys are here.

Having said that, out here you are at the mercy of the elements. No matter what alarms you hear or how prepared you are, you never know what might happen. A trip like this is nothing if not exhilarating!

After packing up the sled Ed and I harnessed the dogs without any problems. Our first day dog-driving by ourselves went swimmingly. We covered 34 miles on the flat sea ice. The snow was thick so we went with little breaks for the ten hours. By the end my back was sore but apart from that it was a great day. We stopped for lunch at a small building out here in the middle of nowhere. Hairy (Theo's nephew), one of the outfitters from Iglulik, teaches children from the village how to hunt out here. He tries to teach them their traditional ways and a bit about their culture. A lot of children are confused between the traditional and modern. They don't know where their identity lies. This teaching is intended to help the children find a purpose and identity.

Another wonderful day. The sun was shining in all its magnificence. After packing up camp I looked towards the horizon to see what looked like a large flat-topped mountain and a cliff face, similar to the edge of the Barnes Ice Cap. After observing it for a while I asked Will about it and without any sense of surprise he said, 'It's a mirage.' How incredible. He has obviously been experiencing these regions for so long that he is accustomed to seeing them. I was awed though. It looked as real as this pen in my hand. A huge cliff face on the flat sea ice. It was like a ghost mountain.

After setting off riding on Abby's komatik we got into a steady rhythm. I lay back floating in between conscious and unconscious, thinking of a million things at one time and then out of my haze came to my surroundings and nothing but the sounds of our komatik creaking in the snow.

The snow was hard packed today and travel was easy. The only obstacles were snowdrifts hardened by the wind and balancing to stay on was the main task. It was like flowing over waves in a sea, except they were frozen. Looking around me with all the space and quiet I saw the twinkling lights. I have seen them before but not like this. As far as the eye could see huge speckles as large as a thumbnail flickered in and out of life as the komatik skated over the surface. As the sun's rays hit the snow they bounced off, creating what looked like a sea of diamonds. It was as if the earth was a giant mirrored ball. I will remember that sight forever. I'm not sure if they are such large sparkles here because of the sea salt, but I presume so.

After a small lunch stop we headed off again. With a bellyful of nuts and the motion of our travel I fell asleep. I wasn't sure quite what had happened but all I remember was being hit by something and I woke up with the komatik riding off away from me on its side. Straight away I realised I was lying on the ground. I jumped up and ran to it to get back on. What had happened was in my sleep I fell off the side and hit my skis, which were at ground level placed horizontally at the back of the komatik. When Simon realised what had happened he couldn't stop laughing! Thanks a lot for the sympathy, Simon! Despite this, we made good mileage today and are only about forty miles from Iglulik. We'll camp tomorrow about fifteen miles from town and spend the day after camped with people coming out to meet us.

We saw a couple more bears sort of wandering about. In camp Abby remarked that polar bear tracks aren't the only prints we've seen in the snow. Caribou, wolf, fox, lemming and arctic hare have all crossed our path at one time or another. If we are observant enough, the tracks can give a good picture of what the animal is up to (running, hunting, eating, denning). More than a few times we have come across the tracks of two different species travelling in the same line (caribou and wolf, fox and lemming). What we realise, if we pay attention, is that we are witnessing predator/prey interaction.

The Arctic is a year-round home to a relatively small variety of animals that have the unique ability to survive a harsh northern environment. I have seen several crows, which seems strange to me. They are quite eerie, black against the snow. Global warming has consequences for animals at all levels of the Arctic food chain, from the krill, to the seal, to the polar bear, and everything in between. Population decline anywhere along the chain has a bigger impact in the Arctic than it might in a warmer climate where there are more animals to fill each niche. The increase in non-native species migrating north is also a concern in the warming Arctic. These non-native species compete with native species for limited resources in an already fragile food web, creating more stress on the ecosystem as a whole.

Again, we were driving under intense UV rays and 24-hour light, directly into the sun, especially in the afternoon. The sun sets around 12 a.m. and comes up at 3 a.m. with just four hours spent behind the horizon, but there's so much reflected light it's bright enough to read a newspaper at midnight. In fact, at 3 a.m. Stetson was reading a book in his sleeping bag, covering up his head, reading by flashlight to get away from the sun. You get tired of it by the evening.

The dogs are positioned around us and the wind has started to howl. We've camped near some open water – a polynya – where seals bathe. It's a lovely spot ... for seals and bears.

Tuesday 8 May
25 miles

I rode with Abby today. We didn't have to make too much ground so there was no rush, except Abby and I fell behind and went nonstop for six hours until we had a five-minute lunch break! To start we rode past the open water with the sun coating the surface with a gold chain-mail blanket. It was stunning. The first few hours we travelled over large hard-packed snowdrifts, which threw the sled from side to side. The second half of the day the ice was as flat as a table for as far as the eye could see. It was fast travelling until the sun melted the top layer of snow, which released the salt it contained. The sky today was awesome, the brightest blue in some areas splattered by moody stormlike clouds. We came to rest on some pack ice. It's safe but there are huge cracks – or leads – in between the different slabs, one leading up to a bright blue iceberg, which went out of the back, and on to the others. I found out that it wasn't that thick when my mukluked leg went through into the water!

There was something of a drama when the dogs were mushed out over the sea ice in the direction we wanted to go. They had to head straight for a deep polynya and then, at the last moment, turn to dash through a narrow bridge. Elizabeth described it later in a despatch.

The trick for the mushers was going to be to get the dogs to run towards the edge of the polynya and then turn right, skirting along its edge, just between Jerry – the *National Geographic* cameraman – and his tripod and the edge of the water. There was no path for the dogs to follow, so Stetson in the lead sled would be telling Whisper, the lead dog, which way to go using 'Gee' for 'right' and 'Haw' for 'left'.

I asked Harry, one of our Inuit friends who met us with our resupply of dog food and fuel, if the ice was thin near the edge. 'Oh yes,' he replied, 'very, very thin.' When Simon and I had fallen through thin ice a few days ago, it was merely an inconvenience. It was a warm day and we were close to shore in shallow water. This polynya, however, was in the middle of a wide stretch of sea ice with deep water below it. I held my breath as I watched the dog-teams approach. They had just left camp and were full of energy. Whisper listened to Stetson's commands and obeyed, but I had to imagine that she was wondering, 'Where are we going?' She turned the team with plenty of time to avoid the thin ice and passed right between Jerry and the ice edge.

In the far distance we could see evidence of even more open water. Dark clouds hung low over the far horizon. We knew that those clouds marked the floe edge, the end of the pack ice and the beginning of open sea. The clouds formed from the water evaporating from the open water and then condensing in the cool air. Like the polynya, the floe edge is another area rich with wildlife. With open water in some places all the year round, there were lots of seals on the ice. This is one reason why Iglulik has been located here for a thousand years – because of rich mammals like seal and fish in the summertime, mostly Atlantic char. We saw several caravans of snowmobiles pulling komatik sleds and kayaks towards the ice edge. We knew they would be coming home soon with seals to feed their dogs and families.

It's our last camp spot – we stay here all day tomorrow and night to finish the last twelve-mile stretch on Friday the eleventh. Stetson's wife Shelly and his son, Nelson, have come out to visit, which he was very happy about. He hasn't seen them for nearly three months. Tomorrow families and sponsors will visit our camp and it will be nice to spend a day with the rest of the team before we head back to civilisation. They're a great bunch of people and I will be sad to leave. No rush for sleep tonight, but I'm off to finish my book!

Wednesday 9 May

Another relaxing day. We woke up at around 9 a.m. this morning and relaxed until about 1.30 p.m. After a morning stroll to wake up, Ed and I chatted. We had a group of sponsors in to visit us from Iglulik, including Fagen, who build industrial plants, and the company Ethanol. Dad has actually got Fagen building two biofuel plants at the moment.

Simon made a small igloo for Nelson to play in, but I spent most of the afternoon in it playing guitar with Simon. Base camp had sent my guitar with the group. What a treat. I was so happy to see it. I had real urges to play while on the trip and it was the longest I've been without a guitar since I started playing properly. Spending the day here was marvellous. We're semi-surrounded by pack ice and small icebergs, like a forest of ice on one side, and the other is a flat, motionless, frozen ocean. The light and sky here are mesmerising.

Everyone got a little silly and larked about having fun. Nelson did a little broadcast. 'Today I went to the top of an iceberg and mined for ice. Skidded down side.' His dad laughed, and said, 'Well, there you have it. Nelson got ice and water off an iceberg.'

Lukie climbed up an ice tower and got us some fresh ice – and watching him, Ed must have been missing the mountains as he also decided to climb the 'iceberg'.

'Ice!' he cried, raising his arms victoriously. He stood on top of the ice block with a chunky pile of freshwater ice down below. At least he thought it was freshwater ice. When he tasted it, however, he found it was quite salty. Lukie hid a smile. Stetson went up to investigate and found that if he cut down deep enough, the ice was indeed fresh. Lukie seemed well aware of this phenomenon and could most likely find fresh water anywhere he chose to camp (another example of skills that come from a culture tied closely to the land). They know the secret of an iceberg floating on a salty ocean. What happens is that salt water doesn't really freeze. Water molecules have to push the salt molecules out of the way in order to crystallise. These salt molecules and a small amount of water form into small pockets inside the ice. The salt water, being heavier than fresh water, then drains down in diagonal and vertical channels to the bottom, and freshwater ice seems to miraculously come from nowhere. However, the top can be salty because of wind-blown brine and spume.

I think everyone was astonished when Will suddenly declared, 'Time for a shower.' He meant a snow bath. Pretty invigorating. But with so many people coming out to see the intrepid explorers, we all decided a little wash and brush-up was in order. Stetson even shaved off his moustache. This evening, another group came in to visit, including Cheryl Teague, one of the first supermodels from the 1960s. All the others remember her from a famous *Sports Illustrated* shoot in a fishnet swimsuit but I've never heard of her. That's what comes of being born in 1985.

Thursday 10 May
second rest day

Now that we have almost reached the end of our journey - in both physical and mental terms - I reflected on some of the lessons that Will had taught me as we had gone along the way. The battle for the planet as we know it is being played out on the sea ice. As the extra energy is being absorbed into the ocean due to human-induced global warming, 80 per cent of that excess energy goes in the ocean and that in turn starts melting the ice – and we're seeing rarer freeze-ups and earlier break-ups. In other words, the ice season, which is so important for hunting and travelling, is starting to diminish. What used to be an eight-month season in Baffin has reduced in some areas down to six months, which makes a big difference.

Overall, the basic statement for the Inuit culture is that it's ground zero for global warming. One of the most thought-provoking comments comes from the Inuit themselves. They say, 'Yes, shorter winter seasons means that we'll have to adapt and make do. Our question to you is, "Can your culture adapt when these changes occur?"'

I went to chat to Will tonight about joining him on his three-month expedition to Ellesmere Island in the deep Arctic. It sounds like a phenomenal project and I will think seriously about joining it. It's a long time, though, and a lot more hardcore. As much as I have enjoyed this one, it will have been a walk in the park in comparison to what Will is proposing. He is a good guy and speaks openly. I don't always know how to react when someone compliments me but he said that I was a real delight to be around, and he was very impressed by how confident I was and how well I fitted in to the expedition and people of any age group. He really feels that I have true leadership potential and as much as I know he would like me to use that to help his passionate cause: global warming. I am still working out what I want to do myself.

Something like this will give me a real platform for knowledge and respect to go and do anything. I feel that already from this trip. It is something I can do on my own, something I can truly be proud of and not have anyone take that away from me.

It is hard. I can see that my dad wants me to get more involved with Virgin and a lot of me thinks the same; but I haven't felt satisfaction in my life like I have in challenging myself on this trip. The next, if I choose to take it on, will be even greater than this. I am only 21 and want to see if I can make something on my own. Not until then can I go on, satisfied to do something through someone else.

It has been an unreal, wondrous adventure. Tonight and tomorrow are the last of the basic routines that break up and fill our day. I'm going to miss them. A captivating silver sun tonight, and I'm going to sleep deeply. My last night, at least for a while, sleeping on a frozen sea.

Friday 11 May
12 miles

Iglulik is located on a small island on the northeastern corner of Melville Peninsula, within the Arctic Circle, about 500 miles north of Hudson Bay. The name 'Iglulik' means 'there is an igloo here' in Inuktitut, and its 1,600 residents are known as Iglulingmiut ('people of the igloo'). It is one of the most traditional Inuit communities in Nunavut and one of the oldest in the north with over 4,000 years of history in one place. I was looking forward to seeing it.

The last day was a full one. After waking at 6 a.m. as normal we packed up the sleds and headed off. Simon stowed my guitar safely away in his wooden grub box and I rode on his komatik. Will was with Luke, Abby with Elizabeth, and Stetson rode with his family and Ed. After about an hour and a half's travel we stopped on a frozen lake about half an hour from Iglulik. A short last day's travel. We waited there for the plane with Dad to arrive. When it arrived Dad surprised me by bringing Mum. She was hiding in the cabin on the snowmobile. I wasn't expecting it.

It was a lovely surprise but it brought home that it was all about to end. I hadn't thought about the end much – I tried not to.

As we rode into town everyone was out on the ice. We went from a sea of ice to a sea of people and it was overwhelming. Everything in town was closed to greet us – schools and businesses alike. The whole population of 1,600 was formed in a semicircle around our arrival area and fire engines were blowing their sirens. It was an incredible feeling, with people everywhere to greet and welcome us for finishing our journey safely. Simon's girlfriend came running up screaming and crying. It was very emotional for them. With the Inuit's close sense of family and community it was a ridiculously long time for them to be apart. Even when Inuit go hunting they take their families.

Everyone was very friendly, welcoming us to Iglulik and asking us how our journey had been. They said it was the biggest thing to ever happen to their home (they all lived in igloos here until the 1960s). The people of these regions have been exploited time and time again and were so grateful to have people there who actually listened to their stories and their wisdom.

After congratulating everyone and being congratulated I went over to Simon's house for lunch. He had been saying all trip that his girlfriend was preparing chicken for his lunch when he got home. I was so excited. On the wall in his house was a banner saying 'Welcome Home'. Will came for lunch as well and it was good. Chicken and vegetables. What a treat to have a home-cooked meal. I went to the bathroom as well and

I remember admiring the novelty of having a sink and a toilet. It's the simple things that are the best!

Simon showed me some photos of him with a dead polar bear, remembering the magnificence of the one that came into our camp, and it reminded me of the culture and hunting way of life that these people live (which must be how we all lived once).

After lunch I went to the hotel and had a shower. What an exhilarating feeling. Half the pleasure was in washing off the build-up of the last three weeks and the other was being naked. Not having clothes on to suffocate my skin. It was probably the best shower I've ever had.

Being inside after spending so much time out in the open was very strange, almost spooky, and it took a while to adjust. Three weeks is the longest I've ever been travelling outdoors. Walking outside relieved the feeling but only temporarily. I remember it feeling quite claustrophobic and dark.

After a last team meeting we all met up at the local community hall where a thousand people came to watch the singer Jewel perform. She has the most beautiful voice and the Inuit loved to hear her play. I was also aware that she had broken a concert tour in Texas, and had paid her own way to come to join us to show solidarity with our aims. Part of this was to do with her roots in Alaska. After her set she asked Simon to play and with a bit of persuasion from the crowd he sang his song. All the time I was dreading getting up and hoping she wouldn't ask me. After Simon performed she said, 'I hear we have another musician in the crowd. His name is Sam and he writes some of his own songs.' My heart sank and my head started pounding. With everyone calling my name, and after promising to myself on the expedition that when the time came I would step up to the challenge, I took off my jumper and walked up onto the stage. Jewel handed me the guitar and I got into position to play. Before I knew it the song was over and I had finished. I sang the first song I ever wrote, 'Momentary Feeling'.

I think it went well. I hadn't played the guitar for weeks and it was the first time I have ever used a mic. Also, performing after Jewel was not an easy task. I remember my leg shaking a bit. The crowd cheered and the white cloud of adrenaline lifted as I walked off. So I'm glad I did it. I faced my biggest fear. Even crossing the frozen, barren planes of the Arctic was easier than getting up on that stage! It's funny what gets to people.

Saying goodbye to everyone was tough and I was sad to be leaving, a lot sadder than I thought I would be. It was a real chapter of my life and I devoted every ounce of my body to it; leaving felt like something was being taken away from me.

As we left I was silent looking out of the window at the world that had been my home for the recent weeks.

Goodbye.

On Necker ...

Sitting here in the tropical heat and lush beauty of Necker, surrounded by a balmy blue sea, is a contrast - but not as much of a contrast to that of my home in London - and I'm glad to have this adjusting period before I travel on to the noise and spin of a city. This quiet, reflective time on Necker is not just a thawing of my body but a thawing of my emotions and time to contemplate and reflect on my magnificent journey.

They had a ceremony in Iglulik yesterday and when they called my name to go up and receive thanks and the plaque they awarded each member of the expedition, the crowd cheered. They were apparently very disappointed when Will told them I had left. It's nice to feel welcomed by a place. That culture is one I will remember for the rest of my life.

Thoughts

Looking back on the expedition and my experiences is a real pleasure. I was so lucky to have the opportunity to see that wondrous place and I'm glad I made the most of every second.

Sitting here in London, a busy city, is a major contrast. It makes me think of the purpose of writing this small book. If anything, I have done it to try and capture my peer group's interest on the important issue of global warming. In a strange way, it is quite an exciting time to live in. As the younger generation, we will see massive changes in our lifetime and hopefully have a chance to stabilise things again for our children.

As a young person, I know how easy it is to see something and be inspired to make a difference, only to be doing something completely different the next minute. If anything, we just need to be aware of the energy we use to do everyday things. Turning on the tap, watching TV, cooking dinner . . .

To acknowledge global warming is to admit that we need to make changes to our daily lives. But they need only be small changes. The effects of global warming, if allowed to develop, will cause us to have to make much, much greater changes, and ones we won't have any choice over. Our voice is the most important thing. Some people say, what difference can I make? But we all know that if everyone in the world put a penny in a box, we would have a lot of pennies. It's not only the difference all individuals together can make, but the pressures our collective voice can put on governments and politicians. Some of their decisions can affect us for the rest of our lives.

In our modern, consumer-based world, we need to choose companies making an effort to be clean. More and more are emerging, which is a good start.

To conclude, I want to say the there are many beautiful and magnificent places in the world, which a lot of us have been inspired by. We all know that overwhelming feeling we get when we see something dramatic in nature. For the balance of this to be destroyed by our laziness would be a real shame. There are clean fuels around today that could power the world we live in. And they're not only cleaner, but more cost effective.

In my mind, global warming is a sort of test to see if mankind can act as one body to change something that will affect all of us. To put aside differences that have been built up over time and realise that we all live under the same umbrella.

I like to think of the arctic as a giant snowflake, amazing in its beauty and magnificent in its structure. But just like a snowflake when it lands on your hand, with a slight change in temperature, it will melt and be lost forever. If we all do our own small part and act like the forks that keep the snowflake intact, it will not melt and disappear. Nor will any other fascinating and fragile places just like it.

The Heavy Stuff

I knew almost nothing about the Arctic when I went there – just the usual stuff, about icebergs and polar bears and that 'Eskimos' lived in igloos. Of course I had heard they preferred to be called Inuit. Like many people I made a mistake about even that, and added an unnecessary 's' to the plural, making it Inuits. But what are Inuk and Inuktitut? What exactly is the difference between a husky and a malamute? Is mush some kind of porridge or slushy snow, or neither? What do they eat? What crops do they grow? I had many gaps in my knowledge.

I had heard that icebergs were melting, glaciers were retreating and that huge chunks were breaking off the Antarctic the size of Texas and floating north into shipping lanes. But I didn't really know why any of this was happening. I have included a few bits and pieces of information in my diary, having learned some of it from incredibly knowledgeable people, like Theo and Simon, who carry a wealth of understanding about the culture in their heads. Later, when I returned home and started to type up my journal, I dug a little deeper. Not too deep – but enough to satisfy some of my curiosity and to get started on what I think will be a continuing interest in the icy world of the people and animals of the Arctic. I have put down some of my research here, lots of cool stuff that has answered some of my questions and I hope will answer a few of yours.

Baffin Island: Land of the Midnight Sun

Quick check

Location: In the Arctic Circle, part of Northern Canada.

Size: 195,928 square miles (507,451 km²). 1,000 miles long (1,500 km). It's the fifth largest island in the world – twice as big as the UK.

Average lowest temperature: -27°C in February (coldest recorded was -54°C).

Average highest temperature: 8°C in July.

Population: 11,000, mostly Inuit.

First settled: 5,000 years ago.

Animals: polar bear, caribou, arctic fox, arctic hare, arctic wolf, lemming, ringed seal, harp seal, bearded seal, walrus, narwhal and whales, especially bow, beluga and killer whale.

Birds: 52 species of migrating birds have been recorded nesting during the summer, including thousand of murres and kittiwakes, arctic skua, tundra swan, snowy owl, snow geese.

Baffin Island

Early sailors said that Baffin Island was so cold it froze the balls off a brass monkey. Most of the island lies within the Arctic Circle, guarding the entrance to Canada's Hudson Bay - which for much of the year is a solid sheet of ice, all the way to the North Pole, 1,500 miles due north. So it's cold even in the summer. I went there towards the end of the long winter and found myself in a world of howling winds, snow and ice, and temperatures that even on the sunniest day never went above 8 degrees below freezing. Believe me, that's cold.

Despite being the fifth largest island in the world, few people know very much about Baffin Island. I wasn't one of those few people. Until I went there, I had barely heard of it and had little idea of its geography and climate. Almost 66 million people live in Great Britain, compared to just 11,000 on Baffin Island in four main settlements along the coast. Yes, it's remote, and wild, bitterly cold and a hard place for a polar bear to survive, let alone a person – yet people do survive and even thrive.

The dramatic heart of the island is the Barnes Ice Cap – a massive, towering remnant of the last ice age. It has been in noticeable retreat since the 1960s, but it is still awe-inspiring. When I actually stood on it, I thought of those explorers of long ago, who had come here in their fragile little wooden ships and stood offshore, gazing upon a mountain of ice over five thousand feet high. The Inuit called the ice cap Auyuittuq – the land that never melts.

Baffin Island was discovered long before 'Columbus sailed the blue in 1492' and discovered America – as we were all taught at school. The first recorded Western explorer to the North Atlantic coast of North America, in around 1,000 AD, was Leif Eriksson – son of a Viking outlaw, known as Erik the Red. The Icelandic Sagas name the place Helluland, which means 'Land of Flat Stones' in Old Norse – the people were called skraelings. Leif Eriksson decided the place was so barren and inhospitable, that he continued further south to a place he named Vinland after the wild grapes he found (now part of Labrador and Newfoundland). The Vikings settled here for a while, built stone houses and picked the wild grapes, thus establishing the Vikings as the first 'settlers' of America, conveniently ignoring those native peoples who were already there.

The search for a shortcut to the Pacific began as soon as Columbus proved that mariners would not fall off the edge of the world, which at the time was believed to be flat, like an inverted saucer. The only routes appeared to be around the storm-tossed Cape of Good Hope (Africa) or Cape Horn (South America), with their fierce currents. It was believed that there was a secret shortcut through the Arctic ice and explorers focussed on that. In 1576 Martin Frobisher, an English sailor, sailed into a narrow bay on the southern shore of what later became Baffin Island.

He landed, looking for gold, the drug that drew so many Europeans to the New World. He thought he'd found some, dug up about two hundred tons of rock, hoping to impress everyone and get rich. But it turned out to be fool's gold – iron pyrite. Instead of finding a great fortune, he got into skirmishes with the Inuit and was stabbed in the buttocks with an arrow. In retaliation, he kidnapped a man and a woman and took them home to England, to be ogled at by the crowds.

By March 1615, a brilliant English navigator and cartographer, William Baffin, was employed by the Muscovy Company – a group of merchants who had a monopoly on trade between London and Russia – to find the legendary Northwest Passage that was believed to be a shortcut across the top of the world to the Pacific Ocean and the treasures of the Orient. He sailed into the huge bay that had already been discovered by Henry Hudson. After noting a great number of whales and other marvels, Baffin's search for the Northwest Passage ended when confronted by '… the Ice so thicke… we turned the Shippes head homewards…'

Interest was rekindled in 1744, when the British parliament offered a prize of £20,000 to anyone who discovered the Northwest Passage. But no one broke through the vast fields of sea ice, though many brave mariners tried; many died and many ships were squeezed by the ice in the different attempts. The only benefits to these missions were that more was learned about the 'Frozen North', and more charts were drawn, which encouraged the arrival of whalers and missionaries. The missionaries replaced the ancient Inuit shamanistic rituals and beliefs with Christianity. The Northwest Passage was finally conquered by sea in 1906 by the Norwegian explorer Roald Amundsen. The island that Baffin discovered now bears his name – but it already had a name: Qikiqtaaluk, the name given by the original Inuit people, who Leif Eriksson had stumbled across a thousand years earlier.

In its two seasons – winter and summer – Baffin Island is extraordinarily beautiful. In the months when the days never end, or the sun hangs low on the horizon, the ice has majestic power; at times blue, at times glowing red and gold. In late June there is a brief summer of some six weeks, when wild flowers bloom, from the hot pink of broad-leaved willow herb, to purple saxifrage that drifts over rocks like fat cushions of glowing colour, the yellow of the Arctic poppy and Arnica, to the shy white bloom of avens. As the summer fades, berries appear that are quickly picked by Inuit women and children to be dried and stored against the long winters – in competition with the summer birds, such as snow buntings, plovers, the snow goose and ptarmigan. The Inuit also hunt the birds to supplement their diet. In a land with long periods of no sun at all it is impossible to grow crops. Almost everything the Inuit eat they hunt for, on the ice or in the sea, which makes for a diet that traditionally is heavy on seal liver, blubber and oily fish. Yet things are changing; Western civilisation is creeping in and today, as the modern Inuit changes with modern society, they are also changing their diet, often relying on manufactured foods that they are not used to.

My own journey across the Arctic ice by sled dog team started on 21 April at Clyde River, a small settlement halfway along the northern shore of Baffin Island. I cut right across the island, crossing the Barnes Ice Cap and heading out onto melting sea ice to my destination's end at Iglulik on the opposite side. The island experiences continuous sunlight for some two and a half months, from 14 May to 28 July. In the winter, the sun sets on 22 November and doesn't rise again until 19 January of the following year year. However, for almost eight months there is a long twilight. So it was that I arrived at the tail end of the long twilight and left at the start of the season of the midnight sun.

The Dope
Things I didn't know about the Inuit

Inuit or Eskimo?
Although it is commonly believed that 'Eskimo' is somehow insulting to the Inuit and Yupik people of the polar regions, the people of Alaska and the easternmost parts of Siberia still refer to themselves as Eskimo. No one is sure where the word originated – nor why it was considered pejorative. It was said to mean 'eaters of raw meat', but now linguists think it means 'netter of snowshoes', which sounds acceptable. Inuit means

'people' – which is also acceptable. Many younger Inuit and Eskimos now just give their personal names when asked what they are, seeing themselves as individuals – which is even cooler. A single Inuit is an Inuk.

Word chain
Seems that Inuit languages make a dialect chain that spreads all the way around the North Pole (the circumpolar regions). That is, each group understands its immediate neighbours, but not the neighbours beyond the neighbours.

Do they believe in ghosts?
Of course – don't we all? Their main ghost is the tupilak, who it seems mostly hung out in Iglulik. It has a human head and parts from different animals – but since it's invisible, only the shaman can see it. It's a dead soul and scares away animals – so the shaman has to scare it away with a knife. Or eat it. Tasty.

Eating ghosts
This was a problem. Inuit religion had rituals that weren't very complicated, but were absolutely necessary. Part of this was that every animal has a soul like a human and it has to be equally respected – but since they ate every animal they respected, it was a major problem. They said, 'The great peril of our existence lies in the fact that our diet consists entirely of souls.' If they didn't perform the right rituals, the ghosts would avenge themselves. They also believed that there were more worlds than just this one. Ghosts could roam around these worlds and return at will.

Do they believe in reincarnation?
Yes – they call it 'Name Soul'. A newborn child was so weak, a recently dead person – an 'old soul' – had to watch over it. The baby was given the old soul's name. If the child spoke, it spoke with the wisdom of the old soul – so people listened and were gentle with the child. If there were no handy newborns around, a puppy was given the dead person's name. If people forgot, or there was no handy puppy around, the dead spirit would return and do mean things.

Where did all this spooky stuff come from?

The northern lights and shifting fogs, sitting around in the dark or under a midnight sun, waiting for caribou herds or sitting near breathing holes hunting seals, gave birth to stories of shadowy phantoms and ghosts that came and went. Could have been a polar bear, of course – silent and deadly. Then staring up at the aurora borealis, or northern lights, persuaded them they could see their dead family and friends dancing in the next life. It sure beats television.

Do they believe in God?

There's Christianity brought to them by missionaries. But they believe in almost everything. People, animals and forces of nature, they all have spirits. If it moves, it has a spirit. Sedna, a.k.a. Nuliajuk, the spirit of the sea, is one of their most important spirits. She lives at the bottom of the sea and controls the sea mammals. It is said that she has a great dog that guards her house – which is why dogs and sea mammals are so important to Inuit culture and survival. As the Danish explorer Knud Rasmussen's Inuit guide told him when asked about Inuit religious beliefs, 'We don't believe. We fear!'

Do they have healers?

Yes – they're called shaman. An Inuit shaman is called an *angakkuq*. *Angakkuit* (plural for *angakkuq*) sometimes become shamans by first becoming sick themselves. While sick, they are imbued with knowledge about all things, including how to cure the sick. They have visions and are able to foretell the weather. *Angakkuit* wore a belt that was a symbol of their powers and used a drum that helped them contact the spirits. The old religion is fading, but all Inuit still remember the songs and drums of the *angakkuit*.

What causes the weather?

Naarsuk, the child in the air, was a giant baby. His giant parents had died in a battle between giants, leaving him to float around the sky. His loosened nappy makes the wind and rain and the shaman has to tie it tight again to change the weather.

Do they all live in igloos?
They did – but not any more. A few hunters build igloos when out and about, or, more often, snow caves (just like a seal or polar bear den). Just as long as the bears don't get confused when they tuck themselves in at night . . .

Have they always lived in igloos, then?
No, once they lived in little houses made of peat sod, whalebone and whaleskin roofs. Once, the Arctic was warm and there was less snow and ice. They hunted bowhead whale and dug peat. Seven hundred years or so ago (approximately 1350) there was a little ice age. No whalebones, no whaleskins, no sod. The Inuit had to find something else to live in before they froze their little mukluks off. Showing great innovation, they invented snow houses – igloos. Really cool. How did they know that a circular shape would be strong and warm?

They have hundreds of words for snow.
Not precisely. They have dozens of complex words to describe different kinds of snow – which is far more precise than our handful of words. We have snow, sleet, frost, hail – and that's about it. They describe it like, 'the kind of big fat snowflakes that fall like goosedown and settles'; or 'little hissy spitty sharp ice like a fine spray from the back of a sled'. (See 'Snow Glorious Snow'.)

They hunt penguins, don't they?
Hardly. Penguins only live at the South Polar regions.

They put their elderly on ice floes to die.
Untrue. They were bumped off rather more speedily. Mostly, when old people wouldn't work or hunt and food was in short supply, their relatives just said, 'Time to die, Pops' – or something close. In other words, they gently suggested that a little bit of euthanasia would tidy up the old igloo nicely. But a far more common thing in desperate times was infanticide. Often the child was wrapped up nicely in furs and a fur cradle and left in a snowdrift. Hopefully, someone without a baby would pick it up and adopt it before a wolf or bear came along. It's important to note that

they don't do this any more. Today, old people are respected as elders, and all children are treated with great love and affection.

What crops do they grow?
None. They have no trees – so no apples or pears, peaches or strawberries. They have never ploughed a field in their lives – so no cereals or rice, porridge, maize, potatoes or cabbages. They live off the land, on country food. This is what they call everything they hunt – which they eat raw (and preferably while still warm when freshly killed). In the short summers, the women and children gather berries, lichens and edible seaweed.

What, no bread or cake?
Flour and sugar were unknown before outsiders arrived. They collected eggs from nesting birds so technically they could have made omelettes – but didn't.

All that blubber and no apple a day must be very bad for you.
All fat, all protein, is the secret of the Inuit diet, years before Dr Atkins came along. Medical researchers have spent years looking at the Inuit diet and they have concluded they are packed so full of nutrients they're healthy. The modern diet of cheap supermarket food many Inuit eat today is causing obesity, diabetes, heart disease and eye problems. There was a recent study that said lack of sunlight and Vitamin D would give them rickets – but doctors found there was more than enough in their diet.

What is throat singing?
It's not gargling. It's a form of wailing that is absolutely unique to the Inuit. It's usually performed by women, who face each other. Drum dancing is also popular. The men drum and dance and the women sing.

What about art?
Inuit artists are very talented. They make carvings out of objects they find around them, like driftwood, walrus or narwhal ivory, soapstone, baleen from whales, skin, bone, stone and antlers. Using these materials, they

have carved and decorated everyday objects. Today, they make drawings and paintings and woven wall hangings, but these forms of art aren't traditional, since their walls were made of ice and they never had paper or canvas or embroidery silks.

The men hunt and the women chew animal skins
They did. Traditionally, men were hunters and fishermen and women's teeth wore down chewing the skins to make them supple and soft enough to stitch into clothing. But widows learned to hunt out of necessity and many women choose to do it today. Men have never offered to chew skins.

Inuit men shared their wives.
Yes. (But no longer...)

No trespassing.
No such thing. They owned no land - it was free to all of the same tribe. Today, the Inuit nation owns the land. Animals belonged first to the hunter or trapper, then to his household.

Sled Dogs

'Sled dogs live to pull.' - John Huston, polar expeditioner and dog musher, 2007.

'Maneraitsiaq's argument was that a dog was a being so far beneath a man that one had no right to scold on account of one of these animals.' - Report of the Fifth Thule Expedition 1921-24 of Knud Rasmussen.

Sled dogs are known as Canadian Eskimo, Canadian Inuit and Quimmik. They are descended from wolves and bred for their speed, stamina and thick coats. They sleep out in the open, curled in a ball, their noses tucked under their bushy tails, never seeming to feel the cold. The most popular breeds are the Alaskan husky, Alaskan malamute, Siberian husky, and the German short-haired pointer. In a race, sled dogs average about 20 miles per hour over distances up to 25 miles.

In 2005, an expedition was organised to re-create the race for the South Pole in 1911–12. The two teams were British, led by Robert Falcon Scott (who happened to be my great-great-uncle) and Norwegian, led by Roald Amundsen. The difference between the two attempts was that the British team man-hauled their sleds, while the Norwegians used dogs. Amundsen won, arriving at the South Pole on 14 December 1911. Scott's team arrived 34 days too late, on 17 January 1912. The re-enactment, filmed by the History Channel and the BBC, wasn't exact, being filmed in Greenland because international agreements ban people from introducing dogs and most other non-native species into the Antarctic.

John Huston – base manager on the Global Warming 101 Expedition that my dad and I went on – was selected as the English-speaking musher on the 2005 Norwegian team, so the Norwegians would remember to speak that language for the cameras. Everything was as close as possible to the original, including the gear used in 1911, from navigating by sextant, to using sealskin clothing, woollen underwear, reindeer sleeping bags, Nansen sledges, and pemmican and blubber for food. An unexpected difficulty was trying to find 48 Eskimo dogs identical to those Amundsen had used. It turned out that the breed was the rarest in the world with only fifty dogs in existence – all on Greenland. They could only get fourteen, for two teams, so on this trip they were very good to the dogs and instead of eating them when they ran short of food – as they had done on the original journey – they fed the dogs their pemmican spaghetti Bolognese.

But what on earth had happened to all the original Eskimo dogs, if there were only fifty left on the planet? Of course, I had to look into it and was quite surprised by the dark story I unearthed.

According to the Inuit, in its great wisdom the Canadian Government, wanting to Westernise the Inuit, sent out the Mounties (Royal Canadian Mounted Police) during the 1950s and 1960s to slaughter some 20,000 sled dogs in Nunavik, in some cases allegedly shooting them in their traces. The Nunavik Inuit have asked for a formal apology and compensation for actions which almost totally destroyed a key component of their culture. The Inuit have collected over a hundred interviews among elders whose dogs were killed. They have collected statements from one hundred elders and witnesses who watched the extermination of entire sled-dog teams. They say that they did not consent to this massacre – which seemed to have been carried out to destroy their culture and make them move from living in traditional igloos to wooden houses in government settlements.

The report also noted that the Inuit were living through massive change at the time, during a period when residential schools were breaking up aboriginal families and denying native children the opportunity of learning about their roots and culture. The Canadian Government supposedly did this to break the Inuit of their culture, which officials said was dangerous in 'civilised' communities.

However, the Mounties totally denied the allegations and their own report absolved them of all charges. According to police records that have survived from that period, both Inuit and RCMP dog teams were ravaged by disease – mainly rabies – sometime between 1950 and 1970 and that is why the dogs were humanely put down.

The RCMP report states: 'The preliminary findings of the review team is that there is no evidence of an organised mass slaughter of Inuit sled dogs by RCMP members in Nunavik and Nunavut between 1950 and 1970.' Some government officials said that resurgent anger over the dog slaughter was partly a long-repressed mourning for a way of life that seemed to disappear overnight. Much of this was to do with military needs, when the Arctic became the front line in the Cold War and the Inuit flocked to work on air force bases and scientific research stations along the DEW (Distant Early Warning) line.

But witnesses who grew up in Iqualuit recalled that hunters had dog teams in harness, ready to go out, when the Mounties shot all the dogs. Some of the people thought if the dogs were tied up and not running loose they would be safe, but the Mounties shot the tied huskies, which were later piled up and burned. Families had to go hunting on foot to survive. Income dwindled and the Inuit had to rely on monthly welfare cheques. Their traditional skills and way of life disappeared. Depression over the situation led to drink, despair and, in some cases, suicide.

The Inuit said that far from being dangerous, the dogs saved the lives of hunters by guiding them home in severe storms, sensed thin ice, rescued hunters when they fell through ice and protected them from polar bears. Older hunters describe how, in the past, when travellers were late to show up, it was assumed that their sled dogs would help them find their way. And they nearly always did.

To fill the gap snowmobile salesmen turned up and families got into debt. It was forty years before dogsledding skills returned to the Inuit, but there are still only about thirty teams instead of the thousands there used to be – and the fuel and exhaust fumes used by the snowmobiles have contributed to the polluting of the pristine Arctic. Authentic sled dogs are now one of the most rare breeds on the planet. Global warming, which has led to a later snowfall and thinner or no ice that heavy snowmobiles fall through, means there is now a big comeback for sled dogs and the latest advice is that the Inuit should turn back to their traditional ways to survive in a changing environment – something that, as I saw for myself, Inuit children are learning at school.

I had seen how dogs sensed thinner ice and how they pulled sleds out of water. I had seen how they warned of polar bears. Noisy machines could warn off game because sound carried for miles in the Arctic environment. Dogsleds are almost silent as they hiss over the snow. Hunting is important for the Inuit diet. The alternative to fish and wild game, such as ptarmigan, caribou or seal, is poor-quality store-bought food that has to be flown in – further polluting the atmosphere. In a land where there are no roads or tracks, dogs can reach almost everywhere across ice and snow. Inuit and their dogs have a symbiotic relationship.

There's nothing like personal experience to tell the story. I saw and fell in love with the sled dogs of the Arctic. I hope they make a comeback.

The thousand-mile dog

Balto was a legendary sled dog. In 1925, the town of Nome, Alaska, was faced with a possible outbreak of diphtheria. Medicine was needed – but the nearest place to find it was in Anchorage, Alaska, nearly 1,000 miles away. The word went out and more than twenty mushers raced their dogsleds in the 40-below-zero temperatures, battling weather and terrain to get the life-saving medicine. Gunner Kassen did it in six days with Balto as lead dog, long before the rest of the pack. Balto was the hero of the hour and became famous around the world. Today, there's a statue to this big-hearted dog outside Anchorage airport. He was an Alaskan husky, very like John Stetson's dogs. The route that Balto took from Nome to Anchorage is now the famous Iditarod dogsled race.

Hitching up

Seals drive sled dogs, one way or another. The harnesses are made of sealskin with a broad chest strap. Lines are also made of sealskin. The gangline loops are threaded on a seal leather strap in front of the komatik, secured with a toggle made from the tip of a walrus tusk. A long, sealskin dog whip snakes in front of the team to keep them from fighting. They are fed five pounds of seal meat a day. Two methods of hitching the dogs are used; the fan hitch is for wide-open spaces and the gang or towline is for enclosed spaces, between rocks or trees.

The fan hitch is when each dog has a separate tugline attached to the sled. The dogs spread out in a fan formation ahead of the sled as they run, and this gives them more room to manoeuvre over rough ice and in areas where dogs may fall through leads or open water. A fan hitch allows only one dog to become immersed and thus prevents each dog from being dragged down. The dog that does fall into the lead is easily rescued. The gangline is a single line to which each dog is attached, usually in pairs, and keeps the dogs in parallel ahead of the sled. Booties, small socklike coverings for the dogs' feet, are used to protect their pads against sharp ice. The sleds are *qamutiit*, singular *qamutiq* in the Inuit language.

Puppy training

Pups are weaned from their mother and placed in their own pen at about six weeks old, so they'll form an early attachment to their musher. They are harnessed and put to the sled at about five months. One method of training is to harness up to a dozen pups behind a pair of experienced older sled dogs and control the speed that they go as they gradually gain in endurance and strength. Mushers say that the dogs' loyalty and desire to please is because they are firm with them and build up an early relationship with them as pups. The poor puppies would have no end of rituals performed on them. Legs were pulled to make them grow strong and fast, noses poked with pins to enhance the sense of smell. Archaeological digs have found skeletons of dogs with compressed fractures of the skull, demonstrating that the custom of extreme severity towards their dogs by the Inuit is a thousand years old.

Mushing

Mushing is a general term for dog power. It implies the use of one or more dogs to pull a sled on snow. Possibly it comes from the French word *marche*, or go, run, the command to the team to commence pulling. 'Mush!' as a command is rarely used now – 'Hike!' is more common in English.

Leader of the pack

Lead dogs steer the rest of the team and set the pace. Leaders may be single or double.

Exceptionally a leader may be unhitched (a loose or free leader) to find the trail for the rest of the team. Qualities for a good lead dog are intelligence, initiative, common sense and the ability to find a trail in bad conditions.

Swing dogs or *point dogs* are directly behind the leader. They swing the rest of the team behind them in turns or curves on the trail.

Wheel dogs or *wheelers* are those nearest the sled, and a good wheeler should have a calm temperament so as not to be startled by the sled moving just behind it. Strength, steadiness and ability to help guide the sled around tight curves are valued qualities.

Team dogs are those between the wheelers and the swing dogs, and add power to the team. A small team may not have dogs in this position. Alternatively, the term may be used to describe any dog in a dog team.

Keep Those Runners Smooth

It is important to make sled runners as smooth and slick as possible so the sled whizzes across the snow without an added strain on the dogs. Before metal or plastic runners, the wooden runners of sleds were kept smooth in a very ingenious way. Two methods were followed (I'm not sure which one is best). One method was to turn the sled over and spread a thick sludge of mixed moss and earth to the base of the runner, allow it to freeze, and then scrape smooth. Water sprayed from the mouth was then smoothed on – layer upon layer – with a piece of wet polar bear hide (ice does not stick to it). This produced a hard, resistant coat of ice. The layer of ice had to be applied often, sometimes several times a day, depending on the distance and terrain to be covered. The route had to be carefully chosen as well; otherwise the hard blows from rocks would chip the coating off. Another method was just to keep painting iced water on the runners with a caribou tail. The layers of ice built up and ice on ice, when the sled gets going, makes for a very fast surface. The sleds on the expedition were specially made by Will Steger's team. The Inuit ones are smaller and lighter and the runners are made from the jawbone of a bowhead whale – which can last for many years.

The Hunter's Boat

The Inuit invented the kayak (Inuktitut: *qajaq* – man's boat) as a super-efficient light and buoyant one-man hunting machine that could skim through waves and turn in its own length without tipping over. It's a perfect stalker, silent and sleek as a shark. If a piece of white cloth was hung up in front, it looked like a drifting growler. Kayaks were made for just one man – and it was said that if a person fell in, or even drowned, he had borrowed someone else's kayak. Typically the length was three times the span of the builder's outstretched arms. The width at the cockpit was the width of his hips plus two fists (and sometimes less). The typical depth was his fist plus the outstretched thumb (hitchhiker). Thus typical dimensions were about 17 feet long by 20 to 22 inches wide by 7 inches deep. This measurement style confounded early European explorers who tried to duplicate the kayak, because each kayak was a little different.

The basic kayak was constructed from stitched animal skins – usually seal – stretched over a wooden frame made from collected driftwood or whalebone. (Archaeologists have found evidence indicating that kayaks are at least 4,000 years old.) Hunters got in fully dressed in their skins and furs, with a sealskin garment on top, an *annuraaq* – from where we get the word anorak. It had a flared skirt that was spread out over the entrance hole and was stitched into place into the sealskin of the frame The seams were then made waterproof with smeared on animal fat, fastening closely in place. Hood and wrists were tightly tied – all making the boat waterproof. If the boat capsized, the hunter had to stay put and spin himself upright. He couldn't afford to land in the water – his heavy garments would have pulled him under and he would have frozen within moments. Instead, the Eskimo roll was invented. The paddles were double-ended and a practised hunter could move at great speed.

An umiak ('women's boat') is a larger open-decked boat ranging from 17 to 60 feet, made with sealskins and wood, allowing entire families and their possessions to move to new quarters. Women paddled with single-bladed paddles, while a man sat aft and steered. It is thought the kayak originally started out as a decked-over umiak and evolved into its now-traditional form. Animal skins (usually walrus) were stretched over a driftwood or whalebone frame that had to be skilfully constructed to provide the strength needed for such a large boat. At between 22 to 33 feet long and about 5 feet wide, umiaks could carry 10 to 15 people, and yet they were still light enough to be carried over ice or land by about six people. In many respects they are close to large coracles, which are of similar construction and equally light. Umiaks are rare today.

Ice

Part of Will Steger's expedition's task was to monitor ice. Through monitoring stations and interviews with local hunters, we hoped to be able to predict when the ice on the rivers and sea is thick enough for safe travel. Weekly ice trail information was posted online. The team also recorded tips from experienced hunters, who have learned to assess the safety and characteristics of the ice, the proximity of river mouths or the salinity of the water. Hunters, for example, related how they picked at ice floes with a harpoon to test for thickness. They explained how ice floes from salted sea water could bounce under your feet like rubber, although it remains safe.

They described how melting ice floes will alternately appear to have white, blue, black or brownish hues, noting that black colours in the first phase of the spring thaw means that the ice is safe, but not in the final phase. The 101 team hopes some of this work will be studied in the classroom so that younger Inuit can learn from their elders for when they go out on the hunting trail. There is no doubt that the Arctic ice is changing – as I saw when we fell through the ice more than once on our journey. In some areas, whole bays and fjords are entirely empty of ice weeks before the usual time, causing havoc for wildlife and sledder alike.

Growlers

Very small chunks of floating ice that rise only about three feet out of the water. When trapped air escapes as the iceberg melts, it sometimes makes a sound like the growl of an animal, and that's how growlers got their name.

Small icebergs, rising between three to thirteen feet out of the water, are called 'bergy bits'. These may be small icebergs in the latter stages of melting, iceberg fragments, or pieces of floebergs or hummocked ice.

Bergy bits may sound cute, but they can still be dangerous to ships because they are harder to see than large icebergs.

A 'floeberg' is a massive piece of sea ice composed of pressure ridges or hummocks (ice that rises up because of movement of the pack ice or the pressure of ice floes jamming and crushing against each other) and which has separated from the ice pack. It may typically protrude up to sixteen feet above sea level.

As the ice pack is frozen sea water, floebergs – unlike true icebergs – are not frozen fresh water and would not make good ice cubes for your drink.

More Icy Terms

Calving – When a glacier breaks off bits it is called calving.

Freshwater Ice – Icebergs are frozen fresh water floating on a salty sea.

Iceberg Alley – Where icebergs from the glaciers of Greenland drift down south, past Baffin Island to Newfoundland and Labrador.

Iceberg Colours – Bergs are usually opaque white because the ice is full of tiny air bubbles, but blue streaks can appear.

Iceberg Drifting – Icebergs may travel thousands of miles from their source on the Polar caps or from glaciers, floating as far as warm Equatorial seas, melting as they go. They are dangerous because when they're found in unexpected places, ships can run into them.

Iceberg Floating – Only between one seventh and one eighth of an iceberg can be seen above water.

Iceberg Furrows – When massive icebergs blow aground they leave deep gouges in the shore and sea bed.

Iceberg Layers – The stripes and different coloured layers in the ice represent different periods of snowfall.

Iceberg Shapes – The basic categories of shapes that are used for iceberg observations. There are two main shapes:

1. *Tabular* – steep sides and a flat top like a plateau.
2. *Non-tabular* – jagged and irregular.

Within both categories are many sub-categories.

i) *Blocky* – like a brick

ii) *Dome* – rounded top

iii) *Wedge* – like a slice of cheese – a steep edge on one side and a slope the other

iv) *Pinnacle* – with one or more spires

v) *Drydock* – geometric, at least one deep almost square indent. Like gaps in teeth or battlements.

vi) *Arched* – as it sounds.

vii) *Valley* – sharp V shape cut into it.

viii) *Weathered* – tabular or non-tabular but messy, dirty, worn out looking.

Iceberg Size – The International Ice Patrol uses various size categories to identify icebergs. (Note: with large icebergs, only about ten percent is seen above water. The rest is floating below, out of sight.)

Growler – less than 1m high and 3m long

Bergy bit – 1–4m high and 5–14m long

Small – 5–15m high and 15–60m long

Medium – 16–45m high and 61–122m long

Large – 46–75m high and 123–213m long

Very large – over 75m high and over 213m long

Iceberg Source – The majority of North Atlantic bergs come from the great glaciers of West Greenland.

Snow, Glorious Snow

As I promised you, there are any number of words for snow – rumour has it anything from a dozen to a thousand. You would have thought, with all the interest in the subject, that someone would have counted them all by now. Here are a handful so you'll get the idea of how one word can sum up some intriguing imagery and nuance.

Aniuk – Snow for drinking water

Aput – Snow on the ground (regular snow)

Aqilluqqaaq – Fresh and soggy snow

▲ Team photo: (top row, left to right) Micky, Will, Ed, Simon, Richard, Sam, Lukie, John; (bottom row) Theo, Elizabeth, Daryl, Abby

▲ The last people you'd expect to bump into in the Arctic – Jeremy Clarkson and James May!

▲ Tent life at dinnertime
- all the mod cons!

◄ A regular map stop
- there's a shortage of
landmarks out here

▲ If the Arctic was a person, I think it would look something like this – an amazingly knowledgeable expert on the Arctic and its people

▼ Me with the wonderful team from the *National Geographic*

Me and my cousin, Otto – our first hour in the Arctic, getting very excited!

Wonderful Inuit children: 'Have you got a girlfriend?!'

How cute is she – a true child of the Arctic!

▲ John is a seasoned expedition pro
  - totally at home in this environment

▼ A war wound . . .

▲ Starting up the frozen river –
what a sight!

▼ Looking at the Arctic through
the Inuit's eyes

As old as time itself - in the foothills of such magnificence we can only look on in awe!

Breaking the ice - Elizabeth trying to stay afloat. This is a problem the Inuit are facing more and more often

Travelling on Simon's sled - feeling pretty cold!

▲ I did it – what a place!

Auviq – Snow brick, to build igloos
Kavisilaq – Snow hardened by rain or frost
Kinirtaq – Wet and compact snow
Maujaq – Deep and soft snow, where it's difficult to walk
Mituk – Small snow layer on the water of a fishing hole
Piqsiq – snow lifted by the wind or blizzard
Qanniq – falling snow

Igloo
Much warmer than a tent, and can be built just about anywhere.

After the key block has been inserted the hut is tightly sealed and a lamp is kindled inside. The heated air, having no exit, begins to melt the face of the snow blocks, which rapidly congeals again on admission of cold air from the outside. Thus each snow block is firmly cemented in place and converted to ice on its inner face. Occupation for a few days then gradually changes the interiors of the blocks, so that the structure is no longer a snow house but a house of ice. The transformation gives it remarkable stability; a man can stand on the summit without causing collapse, and half the house can be destroyed without destroying the other half. Consequently by building a series of intersecting domes and omitting or opening up the common segments, an Eskimo can enlarge a small circular hut capable of housing only one or two families into a community dwelling of three, four or five rooms that will house fifteen or twenty people.

Glance for a moment at the interior of an ordinary, single-room snow hut. You pass with bowed head along a narrow, roofed passage of snow blocks until you arrive at the doorway, a hole at your feet, which you traverse on hands and knees. You rise to your feet. On the right (or left) two feet above the floor is the lamp, a saucer-shaped

vessel of stone, filled with burning seal-oil, and with a
stone cooking pot suspended above it. Behind the lamp
are some bags containing meat and blubber; in front of
it, a wooden table bearing perhaps a knife and a ladle.
A low platform covered with skins occupies fully half the
floor space. There, side by side with their heads facing the
door, the inmates sleep in bags or robes of caribou fur.
If you stand at the edge of this platform, exactly in the
centre of the hut, you can place both hands on the ceiling
and almost touch the wall on either side. A thermometer
three feet from the lamp will register one or two degrees
below the freezing point of water, quite a comfortable
temperature if you are enveloped like the Eskimo in soft,
warm garments of caribou fur.

– Diamond Jenness, Canadian anthropologist, 1900

In my wildest fantasies, I never thought that not only would I help con-
struct an igloo with a real-life Inuit, but that I would also spend time in
one, playing my guitar. Having done all that, I was fascinated to find out
more. When I say it's a really cool subject, I don't mean it to sound like a
pun! But it is – building an igloo is one of the coolest things you can do.

When Martin Frobisher returned to England from his Arctic journey in
1577, he brought with him three Eskimos standing up in their traditional
costumes of fur and skins, a kayak and quite a bundle of authentic hunting gear, from a bow to an ivory-tipped spear. People could see for themselves what remarkable specimens the captives were, like butterflies
pinned to a board. One of the most remarkable things that Frobisher
described was an Eskimo village, built entirely of snow. Unable to bring
a specimen along with him, he did the next best thing – he produced a
drawing. (All this is shown and described in Seyer's Annals of Bristol.)

In a world before television or newspapers, drawings were windows
into exotic worlds. What the viewers saw stunned them into silence. An
undulating collection of scores of snow houses appeared, like molehills,

or frozen beehives covering almost half an acre of ice. They overlapped, one merging with another until it was impossible to see where one ended and another began. 'They are called igloo,' Frobisher said.

One cautious soul asked, 'Where are the windows?'

Frobisher pointed out some small translucent oblongs set into the rounded walls of the snowy domes, one oblong to each igloo, all facing in one direction, where they would get the most light. When it is winter above the Arctic Circle, the sun never rises for three months; light is by stars, moon and aurorae. Frobisher further impressed his audience when he said, 'They use seal gut, stretched out until it is as transparent as a pane of glass. It is dipped into water until it is frozen. And notice how their sleds and kayaks are hung up, so as to keep them from freezing to the ice.'

One man still pressed, 'Where are chimneys? Surely they must have fires or they would all freeze to death.'

No chimneys, Frobisher assured them, explaining that the smoke went out through a small hole in the roof and the interiors of these igloos were warm even when heated with just a small seal-oil lamp. He had also drawn some small one- or two-person hunting igloos that looked strangely like hedgehogs. Someone pointed at the random spikes sticking up, and asked, 'What are those?'

'The Eskimos dig in their spears and knives, which are made of sharp stone or walrus ivory, into the roofs of their houses to keep the white bears away off them.'

In a very short space of time the news of houses made of snow and huge white bears that could eat a man at a gulp were the talk of England.

People have always made their homes out of what materials they have to hand. For thousands of years the ingenious Inuit of the frozen north used blocks of snow in the winters and in the short summers, skins supported over whalebones, peat sods dug from the frozen tundra and, lacking trees, driftwood. It wasn't realised until relatively recently that where stones were available, they used them, piled up to make low support walls and infilled with blocks of peat. The roof was made of caribou skins, stitched together with sinew.

Today, many people are mystified by such questions as: why don't igloos melt; why they don't collapse; do bears try to get inside; and how can one man with no tools other than a knife build a dwelling that can house any number of people from nothing more substantial than blocks of snow?

In the 1950s and 1960s when most Inuit were hijacked away from their traditional way of life and made to settle in prefabricated townships where do-gooders could 'do what is best for them', they almost lost the art of igloo building, along with all their old survival skills. Over thirty years later, when they took back control of their lives, they had to learn all these skills again – either from tribal elders who still remembered, or from academic records. Even today, no Inuit lives in an igloo – though knowing how to build one could make the difference between life and death if they are stuck out on the ice, where they might make a small snow shelter when hunting, or to cover a fishing hole. To keep their culture going and standards up, they have igloo-building contests, as described by Elizabeth Andre, an educational co-ordinator on Will Steger's Baffin Island expedition.

Co-ordinates: 67.00.571 N, 64.39.964 W
Distance Travelled: 13mi / 20.9km
Weather: Wind 5 MPH / 8 KPH, Barometric Pressure 1048 hPa
Cloud cover: clear with a couple of lenticular clouds. Some alto cirrus clouds in late afternoon.
Sunrise: 6:12 a.m.
Sunset: 6:41 p.m.

I was cutting ice chunks with an axe to weigh down the snow flaps on our tent when I looked up to see Simon cutting large snow blocks with a saw out of a snowdrift. I asked him what he was doing and he replied, 'Building an igloo.'

This would be the first time on this trip anyone had built an igloo, so I was curious and ready to help. In between taking photos, I carried blocks of snow over to the steadily growing igloo and passed them over the wall to Simon. Simon would quickly cut them to size with his snow knife and expertly fit them into place. He was so speedy that I barely had time to run back to grab another block before he was finished with the previous one.

At one point we had used all of the blocks Simon had cut. Simon was still busy shaping the most recent block. I thought I would try my hand at cutting a snow block out of the drift. It was not nearly as easy as Simon had made it look, I soon discovered. The block I cut was not quite the same shape and size. Simon came over to look and we both had a good laugh. Simon quickly cut another stack of blocks and we were back to work on the igloo in no time.

The base of the igloo was large enough that two people could sleep comfortably on its floor with a stove for warmth between them. The ceiling was high enough for a person to stand inside. The door was just big enough for a person to wriggle out, but small enough to keep the cold wind from coming in.

I thought how cosy the igloo would be — much more so, I imagined, than our thin-walled nylon tents. Snow is a good insulator because of all the air space in it; just like the fibreglass insulation in modern homes. I also thought about all the Arctic animals that make their own snow-dens so they can be comfortable in these extreme weather conditions. I thought about the polar bears and cubs in their dens, the voles in their snow tunnels, and the seals and pups in their snow dens on top of the sea ice. Without snow for shelter, life would indeed be difficult with the

Arctic winds and sub-zero temperatures. I have heard reports of poor snow conditions leading to collapses in certain local populations of voles. These voles are a food source for arctic fox and other animals. If there are not enough voles, then the fox populations decrease as well.

Now that I have had a chance to experience the bitter cold and the sometimes-unrelenting winds of the Arctic, I can begin to have an appreciation for the value of a good shelter. I can begin to understand the necessity of good snow for the animals that make the Arctic home.

When Simon and I finished building the igloo I cut a few more pieces of ice to make a windbreak for Frank, one of our short-haired lead dogs, just in case the wind picked up in the night.

— Elizabeth Andre

An Igloo Builders' Guide

The people of the frozen northlands of Canada and Greenland have many words to describe snow. One of the most important is the type of snow suitable for building an igloo. The word igloo is derived from the Inuit word *igdlu*, meaning house.

1. Location: A flat field of hard snow, suitable for cutting building blocks.
2. Temperature: Below freezing (32°F/0°C)
3. Tools: A snow spade and a saw. In olden days these implements would have been fashioned from bone.
4. Check the direction of the wind – you don't want a blizzard blowing straight at the entrance.
5. Foundation: Scrape and clear a circle of the size required. Some Inuit build around the hole from which they have taken the blocks. Ten to fifteen feet

in diameter is about right for an igloo to hold two to three people.

6. Using the tools, cut large oblong snow blocks, about two feet by four feet, for the base. The blocks should be solid enough that they can be carried without breaking. Place them neatly along the perimeter of your circle. The edges of the blocks should be shaped and angled towards the centre, to start the gentle curve of the dome.

7. Cut progressively smaller snow blocks as the igloo grows. Standing the blocks in the wind will harden them and strengthen them.

8. Work in a spiral, placing the new block just ahead of the block below. Repeat the slight angle towards the centre. The weight of the blocks supports one another and contributes to the stability of the structure.

9. Stuff cracks between the blocks with snow as the walls build. The smaller cracks between the blocks can be smoothed over but two or three cracks should be left unfilled to provide adequate ventilation. Snow that piles up inside the igloo during the construction process should be cleared away before the snow dome closes as its removal is easier this way than trying to shovel it out the entrance.

10. The height of the igloo will equal your reach. After the final block is wiggled and shaped until it wedges into the top from the inside, the snow dome is complete. A livable igloo can be built in three to six hours.

11. Dig out the entrance tunnel beneath the igloo floor. Make it as small as possible to deter curious polar bears. Put a bend in it so snow won't blow in.

12. Put several blocks along one wall as a sleeping platform.

13. When the igloo is sealed light a small fire or lamp inside. The heat begins to melt the interior of the snow blocks, which quickly turns into ice. As this

pattern of freezing from the inside out repeats itself for a few days, the igloo transforms from a snow house into an ice house of tremendous stability. With warmth inside the igloo, the surface of the walls will melt and freeze over, to form a smooth, airtight ice surface. The roof over the entrance tunnel prevents snow from blowing into the igloo. The lamp seasoning, a week to a month of melting and refreezing, gives igloos their great physical strength by turning the snow blocks to ice from the inside out.

14. Hot air from your body and the stove rises and is trapped inside the dome. (Just the heat from your body will make a properly built igloo warm.) Cold air falls into the sink and flows away to the outside. It is essential to cut ventilation holes in the walls with an ice axe.

15. A full-grown man can stand on an igloo without it collapsing and a properly built igloo can withstand hurricane-force winds. But even an igloo cannot withstand the summer Arctic thaw. In areas where four- or five-room igloos were permanent shelter, the snow domes needed to be rebuilt every winter. (Caribou-skin tents or sod houses were used for the summer.)

16. A temporary shelter can be made by simply laying snow blocks around in a circle on the surface. A single hunter or small group might build these far out on the winter sea ice.

Warning! Without ventilation, lethal carbon monoxide will build up.

Inuksuk

A stone marker that Inuit built as landmarks on the tundra. Some *inuksuit* (plural) were built to resemble humans, to help hunters lead caribou into lakes where they could be more easily killed from a *qajak* (kayak).

Seasons in the Arctic

Spring
The sun rises at the North Pole on the spring equinox, approximately 21 March, and the sun rises higher in the sky with each advancing day, reaching a maximum height at the summer solstice, approximately 21 June.

Shadows cast in May are long, because the sun is low in the sky. In June, near the summer solstice, the shadows are short because the sun is higher in the sky.

Summer
The North Pole stays in full sunlight all day long throughout the entire summer (unless there are clouds), and this is the reason that the Arctic is called the land of the 'Midnight Sun'. After the summer solstice, the sun starts to sink towards the horizon. In summertime, the sun is always above the horizon at the North Pole, circling the Pole once every day. It is highest in the sky at the summer solstice, after which it moves closer to the horizon, until it sinks below the horizon, at the autumn equinox.

Autumn
At the autumn equinox, approximately 21 September, the sun sinks below the horizon, and the North Pole is in twilight until early October, after which it is in full darkness for the winter.

Winter
The darkest time of the year at the North Pole is the winter solstice, approximately 21 December. There has been no sunlight or even twilight since early October. The darkness lasts until the beginning of dawn in early March.

Some Inuit words
Li (EE) – Yes
Akaa (ah-KAH) – No
Kinauvit (kee-NOW-beet) –What is your name?
Sam Branson Uyunga (OO-YOO-nga) – My name is Sam Branson
Qanuiput? (Ka-noo-WEE-peet) – How are you?
Qanuingittunga (KA-no-WIN-ngi-TOO-ngah) – I'm fine
Igvili (IG-vee-lee) – And you?
Ikee (Ik-KEE) – It's cold!
Okho (oh-KHOE) – It's hot!
Puyuk (POO-yook) – Beautiful
Qujanamik (kko-YAA-na-mee) – Thank you
Nagligivagit (na-GLEE-ghee-va-geet) – I love you
Iilali (ee-LA-lee) – You're welcome
Sunouna (soo-NOW-na) – What is it?
Igdlu – house
Qapsituqpa (kap-SEE-took-pa) – How much does it cost?
Atii (a-TEE) – let's go
Suva (SOO-vah) – What?
Taima (tay-MA) – That's it! (finished)

Making Fire

This text was originally published in 1907 by the Bureau of American Ethnology as part of its *Handbook of American Indians North of Mexico*. It was later reproduced, in 1913, by the Geographic Board of Canada. I have cut out references to other tribes, and just left the fire-starting methods of the Inuit. It never occurred to me to wonder how, in all that snow and ice, the earliest Inuit managed to start a fire. Obviously, though they didn't do a lot of cooking, they did have oil lamps.

Two methods of making fire were in use among the American aborigines at the time of the discovery. The Eskimo [Inuit] practised the first method, by flint-and-pyrites (the progenitor of flint-and-steel). The second method, by reciprocating motion of wood on wood and igniting the ground-off particles through heat generated by friction, was widespread in America, where it was the most valued as well as the most effectual process known to the aborigines. The apparatus, in its simplest form, consists of a slender rod or drill and a lower piece or hearth, near the border of which the drill is worked by twisting between the palms, cutting a socket. From the socket a narrow canal is cut in the edge of the hearth, the function of which is to collect the powdered wood ground off by the friction of the drill, as within this wood meal the heat rises to the ignition point. This is the simplest and most widely diffused type of fire-generating apparatus known to uncivilised man. Among the Eskimo [Inuit] the simple two-piece fire drill became a machine by the use of a hand or mouth rest containing a stone, bone or wood socket for the upper end of the drill, and a cord with two handles or string on a bow for revolving the drill. By these inventions uniform and rapid motions and great pressure were effected, rendering it possible to make fire with inferior wood. The four-part drill consisted of two kinds: (a) The cord drill, which requires the co-operation of two persona in its working, and (b) the bow drill, which enables one person to make fire or to drill bone and ivory. The distribution of these varieties, which are confined to the [Inuit] and their neighbours, follows no regular order; they may be used together in the same tribe, or one or other may be used alone, although the presumption is that the cord drill is the older. The Eskimo [Inuit] prized willow catkins as tinder. [N.B. They collect it in the short summers and store it for use in the winter.]

The Kudlik – a Multipurpose Lamp

A kudlik (*qulliq*) is a crescent-shaped open lamp carved from stone and filled with blubber oil. A wick made of moss or Arctic cotton draws the oil to make a type of liquid candle. Small though they were, these lamps were used by the Inuit to light and heat tents or igloos, melt snow for water, dry clothing and cook food. A very small amount of heat was enough to warm the igloo sufficiently to dry clothing. The steam would condense on the walls of the igloo and turn to ice. Arctic cotton is a type of grass that produces silky white plumes that resemble cotton balls. Inuit children picked the cotton in the summer for use as wicks and mattress stuffing.

Food – for Arctic expedition travel
Co-ordinates: 69.44.976 N, 76.47.051 W
Distance Travelled: 33mi / 53km
Weather: Temp 6°F / −14°C, Wind 10 MPH / 16 KPH
Cloud cover: Clear skies
Sunrise: 3:19 a.m.
Sunset: 11:06 p.m.

After 71 days of trail food, our thoughts start to wander towards a few small novelties we'd love to taste. For me, a simple mango would suffice. Elizabeth reports that a peach would be just lovely. Each of us is starting to crave a little something more than the rice, pasta and oatmeal that have become the staples of our diet. Tonight it is cheesy rice, a trail classic and a favourite of John Stetson's (who seems to make it every night). Boil a little rice, add butter, a few chunks of cheese, mushroom soup mix and presto! You're done. Mmmmm, good.

Lately, since the days have gotten warmer, we have adapted our cheesy rice recipe to meet our waning appetites. At the start of the trip I added at least three large chunks of buttery goodness to my rice (and heaped three more onto a toasted piece of bread, which I ate beforehand). Honestly, I was often tempted, when the temps got down to minus forty, to eat a few extra chunks plain, just waiting for the rice to boil. These days butter has lost some of its lustre. While I still add a bit to my oatmeal, it's just not as tempting as it used to be.

The reason, of course, is that our bodies crave the nutrients we need. We burned a lot of calories during the first half of the trip, just staying warm. 'Food is fuel', I've heard it said, and couldn't agree more! As the temperatures warm it takes less energy to warm our bodies and thus we crave less of the high-calorie foods.

We're not the only ones travelling through the Arctic, adapting our diet to the changing environment. The arctic fox, whose tracks we've seen weaving back across our own, has adapted in a particularly useful way. With their thick winter coats and slow metabolism, the arctic fox rarely has to change its summer eating habits at all in the winter months. Fox are able to feed as normal, hunting lemmings and voles, until the temperature drops below minus forty, at which point they need to consume more food than normal to stay warm.

We are all a little leaner than we began, thanks to the cold weather and constant exercise. Butter is still on the menu as we have five more days until we reach Iglulik, and are averaging thirty miles a day. And have I mentioned chocolate? We're still quite happy with our chocolate, at thirty above or thirty below.

Bon appetite!

Abby

In The Hood

Inuit make clothes and footwear from animal skins, sewn together using needles made from animal bones and threads made from other animal products. The Inuit skin parka has travelled to Europe, where it is generally made of lighter fabric, stuffed with down. Some are just oilskins – but the shape is the same as the Inuit skin one. Snug as a bug ...

Living in the coldest place in the world has taught the Inuit the secret of keeping warm. People who travel there with the best quality, the most expensive down parkas and insulated boot are astonished to find that the traditional clothing is warmer, lighter and more windproof. It's hardly surprising that it's the warmest clothing in the world. If it works for animals in temperatures as low as sixty below, it works for humans.

The Inuktitut word for their traditional garments is '*Annuraaq*', which literally means 'an article of clothing'. It's also where our word 'anorak' comes from. It is made of skins and furs and consists of watertight boots, double-layer trousers and the parka, a tight-fitting double-layer pullover jacket with a hood. The inner layer of the parka has fur against the skin and the outer layer has fur on the outside. Each layer traps air and acts as insulation. Sinew thread and bone needles were used to sew the skins into warm and watertight clothing, but today, waxed tailor's thread is often used and steel needles. The edge of the hood is usually finished with a fringe of fur from animals like the wolf or wolverine. The luxurious glossy hairs of the furs enable ice or snow to be shaken away and help to stop draughts creep in around the face. The hoods of Inuit women's parkas – *amautiit* (singular *amauti, amaut* or *amautik*) in Inuktitut – were traditionally made extra large, to protect a baby from the harsh wind when snuggled against the mother's back. Caribou is the best fur. The hair is twice as dense as that on sealskin, and a thick layer of hollow guard hairs also encloses air. Styles vary from region to region, from the shape of the hood to the length of the tails.

Some level of superstition also plays its part in what is worn when. The success of the hunt depends on skill and respect – respect shown to the animals being hunted. When hunting sea animals like seals, a hunter would wear boots, (kamik or mukluk) made of sealskin, and designs varied for men and women. When hunting on land, a hunter wore boots made of caribou skin. These taboos were partly in order not to offend the spirits of the animals, but there was a logical reason behind the superstition. Boots made of sealskin were best when hunting on ice because they were warm, durable and water-resistant. Caribou-skin boots got wet more easily than sealskin, but because of the thick, dense fur, they were warmer in the snow. During the short summer season, Inuit also live in tents made of animal skins and bones when travelling or hunting.

Sunday 6 May - Keeping in the Heat
Co-ordinates: 69.51.114 N, 78.11.071 W
Distance Travelled: 34.16mi / 54.98km
Weather: Temp 3°F / −16°C, Wind 10 MPH / 6 KPH,
Barometric Pressure 1059 hPa
Clear skies
Sunrise: 3:17 a.m.
Sunset: 11:07 p.m.

Have you ever taken a nap sprawled out on top of a moving dogsled? I did today as I rode with Lukie. Lukie prefers that his dog-teaming companions ride instead of ski, and I was happy to take a break from skiing.

The one downside of riding instead of skiing is that it is easy to get cold. When I'm skiing I often stay comfortably warm in just a few light layers, even on the coldest of days. My goal when skiing is to not break a sweat. To do this, I shed layers just before I start to overheat. Then when we stop for a snack break, I don my big coat to keep warm until we start moving again.

When riding, in contrast, I wear my several long-underwear layers, a wool sweater and my big puffy coat. This morning, however, even with all these layers on, I was feeling cold sitting on Lukie's sled. The temperature was a bit cooler than it had been for the last week or so and there was a strong breeze in my face. The muscles in my back tensed up and I could feel my core temperature starting to fall. I knew soon, if I didn't take some action, I would start to shiver. The sled was moving too quickly, however, for me to try to warm up by running alongside through the deep snow.

'How do the animals who live in the Arctic do it?' I asked myself. Then I remembered watching our sled dogs curl up in snowstorms and tuck their noses under their tails. Their tails trap the warm, moist air they exhale and then warm and humidify the air before they breathe in. Arctic land animals like polar bears, musk oxen and caribou also have noses that are well adapted to the cold. Their noses warm and humidify the air the animals breathe.

A human, on the other hand, can lose more than half of the heat his or her body produces each hour just by breathing in cold, dry air. Our bodies have to spend a lot of energy to heat that air and humidify it, but then we lose all that heat energy when we breathe the air back out.

Luckily for me today, I had a BreathXChange mask handy. It is made of wind-stopper fleece and fits snugly around my head, face and neck. Over my mouth it has a filter that, much like the nose on a polar bear, traps the heat and moisture from my exhalations and warms and humidifies the air I breathe.

I put on the mask and pulled my hood with the fur ruff tightly around my face. Soon I was warm enough to start to feel relaxed, just like a polar bear basking in the sun. The gentle rocking and lurching of the sled as it glided silently over the snowdrifts soon made me sleepy. I leaned back on my backpack, closed my eyes and had some Arctic dreams.

Elizabeth

Polynyas

Polynyas are naturally occurring areas of open water surrounded by sea ice. They can vary in size from less than a few square kilometres to immense areas over 50,000 square kilometres. In the Arctic, the ice pack surrounding polynyas is over six feet thick, and without these open areas, air-breathing creatures like seals, walruses, narwhals and belugas would drown. Polynyas perform a valuable role – but they also are a place where killer whales and polar bears lie in wait to hunt vulnerable prey.

The holes are kept open by an upwelling of warmer water ($-2°C$) caused by a variety of factors – currents or topography. This warmer water constantly melts the bottom of the ice and the constant flow keeps it from reforming. In spring, the penetration of light leads to a sudden blooming of microalgae, the basis of the marine food chain. Up the chain, plankton thrives, bringing arctic cod, which diving marine birds, seals and whales feed on – all the way up the chain to the Inuit and polar bears. Polynyas are great places both for hunters and naturalists.

Legends of the Aurora

'Here, they are constantly playing ball, the Eskimo's favourite game, laughing and singing, and the ball they play with is the skull of a walrus ... It is this ball game of the departed souls that appears as the aurora borealis, and is heard as a whistling, rustling, crackling sound. The noise is made by the souls as they run across the frost-hardened snow of the heavens. If one happens to be out alone at night when the aurora borealis is visible, and hears this whistling sound, one has only to whistle in return and the light will come nearer, out of curiosity.' – An account of Greenland Eskimos collected by Danish-Inuit explorer Knud Rasmussen in 1932

Auroras have inspired awe and fear since living memory. The entire sky is filled with pulsating, shimmering colours like a living painting between earth and sky. The colours and writhing shape change so fast they seem to resemble fantastical creatures – the creatures of legends.

The Inuit of the Hudson Bay regions believed that auroras were the spirits of the dead that would be attracted by whistling. Before the spiralling ghostly shapes came too close, a handclap or clicking your nails could send it away. Others said the aurora was produced by spirits playing a game of celestial football with a frozen walrus skull – while the Inuit of Nunivak Island said it was the spirits of dead walruses playing football with human skulls. Children were warned to come in after dark or the spirits would take their heads to use for these games in the sky.

To some Eskimo groups, the aurora was an indicator of good weather. Alaskan Eskimos, though, said it was malevolent, and they wouldn't leave their igloos without weapons when it was present. It was said, 'He who looks long upon the aurora soon goes mad.'

Every culture of the Far North has its own legends. The Finns called the aurora 'foxfire', and said it was caused by gigantic fiery foxes that lived in Lapland brushing their flaming tails back and forth across the arc of the sky, turning it to fire. Seeking a more scientific explanation in unscientific times, the Norse – who depended on herring fishing – said it was 'herring flash', caused by vast shoals of herrings reflected off ice and the sea into the sky. More traditional Norse mythology said that the aurora was a flaming arch, named Bifrost, over which the gods travelled between heaven and earth. Or it was Rutja, the river that flowed through fire and divided the realms of the living from the dead.

The colours vary from predominately yellow, green and blue to a vibrant, fiery red or intense, luminous purple. When the sky was red, the Vikings said it was *vigrod*, the colour of war paint. Sometimes it was described as lights carried by the Valkyries as they rode the sky – a similar tradition to some tribes of North American Indians, who said it was the light of lanterns carried by spirits seeking the souls of dead hunters, or the fires of medicine men. There was even some overlapping of Viking and Inuit culture, brought about when the Vikings travelled between the Arctic, Greenland and the land that became Canada. In the Arctic regions the phenomenon is called the aurora borealis – 'the northern lights'; while in the Antarctic it is known as the aurora australis. All Arctic and Antarctic cultures worldwide have their own story. Australian aborigines say it's their gods, dancing across the sky. The Chinese and Northern Russians describe them as serpents – and this is where the Chinese dragon mythology probably originated.

Nobody really knows how or when the various myths spread, although there is a great similarity in them. It's possible they started in China with dragon legends and spread eastwards across the Bering Strait, when it was still a bridge that joined America with Asia, when the first peoples arrived in what is now Alaska. Possibly, the mythology also travelled the other way, via the Mongol hordes to Finland, Lapland and Scandinavia - and from there to Greenland, Newfoundland and Eastern Canada.

Today, most Inuit and Eskimos say the stories are just fanciful mythology, but still the stories linger, with some added ones. In modern times it has been said that the aurora is caused by icebergs crashing into each other, while Klondike gold prospectors said it was the reflection thrown up by the elusive mother lode that was just within their grasp.

On those Arctic nights when the common auroral arch seems to expand, break up and dance overhead in myriad flaming colours, one experiences a mild electric shock about the ears and hair that is easily distinguished from the nipping of the frost. The air becomes heavily charged with ozone, which penetrates the nostrils like chlorine and suggests the smell of blood at a fresh kill. A muffled, swishing sound accompanies these displays. Small Eskimo boys band together and frolic about on the snow attempting to imitate the ominous sounds from overhead. It would be difficult, indeed, to convince these small boys that they weren't hearing anything. No doubt the muffled sounds heard in the silent Arctic night are actually reverberations of tremendous claps of auroral thunder many miles above the earth.

There seems to be a relationship between the aurora and the weather or, strictly speaking, the winds. If it is calm and very cold, the arch is low. As the wind comes up, the arch rises, and if it approaches a gale, the arch seems to break up at times.

'There's Magic in the Arctic'
– E. L. Keithahn, one time curator of the Alaska Territorial Museum, in the July 1942 issue of *The Alaska Sportsman*

Nothing was known about what caused the aurora itself until relatively recently; while the sounds still remain something of a mystery. Are they real or imagined?

According to Canadian anthropologist Ernest Hawkes, who published an account in 1916, 'The whistling, crackling noise, which sometimes accompanies the aurora, is the voices of spirits trying to communicate with the people of the earth. They should always be answered in a whispering voice.'

Tom Hallinan, a professor of geophysics at the Geophysical Institute, said he's heard the aurora and has talked to many others who have heard its strange, unearthly whisper. 'There's something going on. It's scientifically unreasonable, yet people do hear it.'

According to Professor Hallinan, the thin air of the ionosphere can't carry sound waves – and even if it could, we're so far away that it would take several minutes for the sound to reach us. Possibly the brain senses electromagnetic waves from the aurora and somehow converts them to sound. Another theory is that electrical currents induced on the ground by the aurora (which also corrode the Trans-Alaska oil pipeline) may create an audible electrical discharge from nearby objects such as spruce trees or buildings.

Those who hear the sound of the aurora are convinced it's real. They describe it as swishes, hisses, sizzles, rustles, rushes, whizzes, crackles or whispers. It can sound like the tearing of silk, the wind in the trees, the noise of flying birds, the sweeping of sand or the flapping of a ship's sails. But many remain sceptical, especially in light of an eighteenth-century experiment. David Thompson, an explorer for the Hudson's Bay Company, blindfolded his companions during a display because he thought their eyes were deceiving their ears. Sure enough, the sightless men stopped hearing the noise. Over the centuries, other polar explorers – such as John Franklin who discovered the Franklin Passage named after him – never mentioned any sound. However, the polar explorer John Richardson, who had never heard as much as a whisper, crackle or hiss, said he believed they existed because 'the uniform testimony of the natives ... induces me to believe that its motions are sometimes audible'.

Perhaps the conditions must be right before sound is heard – and only those who live in the far north and far south are there at the right time. It could be the wind, it could be the cracking of ice, or the far off sound of 'auroral thunder' – or it could all be in the imagination as David Thompson said.

How the aurora is formed

The aurora dances between sixty and two hundred miles above the surface of the earth – but what causes this display of such gigantic proportions?

Scientists are still out on this – but in its simplest terms, the sun switches on the northern lights, like a celebrity switching on Christmas lights. The oldest theory has it that when solar flares shoot into space, high-energy-charged electron and proton particles travelling for some days at about 900,000 miles an hour – slower than the speed of light – collide with gases in the earth's atmosphere. A cloud of these particles is called plasma. The stream of plasma coming from the sun makes solar storms and winds. As these solar winds collide, or interact, with the edge of the earth's magnetic field, some of the particles begin flowing around the earth and become trapped in the Van Allen belts that are held in place by the earth's magnetic field. These radioactive belts consist of highly energetic ionised particles of electrons and protons (plasma) trapped in the earth's geomagnetic fields. It is when the particles collide with the gases – oxygen and nitrogen – in the ionosphere that they glow and fluoresce as the aurora.

A more recent theory is that auroras are manifestations of solar coronas. The solar surface boils and seethes on a titanic scale, and the magnetic fields embedded within it are incessantly shifting and twisting in conjunction. This great roiling activity brings oppositely directed magnetic fields together until they annihilate one another, releasing X-rays and energetic particles. Usually this leads to the eruption of a solar flare – but if there's a titanic magnetic upheaval, it will produce an event of majestic splendour – a coronal mass ejection, often covering a quarter of the sun's surface. Their great speed and the strength of their magnetic fields are what generate large solar storms and dramatic auroras.

Green and shades of yellow, the most common colour, occur at an altitude of about 100 kilometres. Shades of blue are there as well, but the human eye doesn't see it easily. When the incoming particles are especially energetic, they create red light on the lower edges of aurora at about 80 kilometres, but the rarest auroras of all – a hugely dramatic all-red or even electric purple curtain that covers the entire sky – occur much higher, at 300 to 500 kilometres altitude, and are associated with a large influx of electrons. These electrons are moving too slowly and have less energy to penetrate deeply into the atmosphere. When the coronal hole faces the earth it is like looking down the barrel of a gun that fires northern lights. Little wonder that the ancients were awed and terrified.

In a typical auroral display, the light is a mixture of many colours. There's actually a fair bit of blue, but the human eye doesn't pick it up very well. We see much better in the green part of the spectrum, and there is a strong yellowish-green component in the light of a typical aurora, so we often see green displays.

Mirages, frost quakes, will-o'-the-wisps and sun dogs
Mirages aren't seen only in deserts; they are often seen in the polar regions, as E. L. Keithahn described:
'I recall seeing a beautiful, four-masted schooner appear one morning about two miles offshore ... sea littered with floe ice. And then, right before my eyes, it simply faded out. This kept on intermittently for four days; then the real ship did pull into the roadstead, dropped its hook, and the natives went out in their umiaks to barter. When the trading was completed we saw that same ship sail proudly away to the north on the very tip of the masts! It was another antic of mirage.'
On frost quakes:
'It appears the earth can stand just so much freezing, then, due to expansion, something has got to give. As the earth cracks there is a local earthquake, giving the

occupants of an igloo directly over it quite a scare, yet not even disturbing their next-door neighbour.'

On the Arctic will-o'-the-wisp:

'It's a ball of fuzzy light about the size of a small haystack that silently plunks down in front of you some nights when you are walking along, disappears like magic, appears perhaps behind you, glows with a cold, white light, then bounces away. Now visible, now invisible, it appears and reappears as if it were too hot to alight and not sure it existed anyway.'

Keithahn also mentioned other unusual phenomena such as sun dogs and light pillars, which are readily explainable, as are the frost quakes and mirages. But some things will remain mysteries – such as the Arctic will-o'-the-wisp and stories of narrow white paths through the snow suddenly extending before people on pitch-black nights to entice them home or towards the unknown.

The big fridge

Arctic animals have found clever ways to survive in below zero temperatures for over eight months of the year. Most of them eat tons of fat, which builds up a thick layer of blubber – and blubber is good insulation. Many of them, like polar bears, arctic wolves and muskox, have developed the layered look. They grow thick coats with two layers – the inner layer is dense and fluffy and the outer layer is made up of 'guard hairs' that trap any body heat that escapes and, at the same time, insulate against cold air getting through.

Ringed seal: Named after the dark rings with light circles that cover its body. It's the smallest and most common marine mammal in this part of the Arctic. (Worldwide there are 19 types of seal.) During the winter, ringed seals make breathing holes through ice up to 8 feet thick by visiting each one often, and keeping the hole open and free from ice. In March, a female enlarges one of the breathing holes that has snow over it to make a small igloo, where she whelps one or two pups. The pups can swim by three weeks. Polar bears can smell these seal dens from miles away. They break through with their sharp claws to swallow the baby seals in a few gulps.

Harp seal: Named after the black, harp-shaped saddle on its back. Like all seals, harp seals can stay underwater for thirty minutes at a time. They're fast swimmers and this helps them to escape their main predator, the polar bear. In late winter, females climb onto a chunk of ice to give birth to fluffy white pups. Pups have no blubber at first, so need their warm coats – but they get fat fast, gaining over 80 pounds in just three weeks on mum's rich milk.

Bearded seal: Distinguished by long, drooping whiskers. Like walruses, bearded seals are bottom feeders and eat crustaceans, molluscs, worms, hermit crabs and clams.

Harbour seal: Also known as the common seal, it is grey with dark blotches and relatively tame – hence its name.

Arctic char or charr: Related to both salmon and trout, with a firm, pink or bright red flesh and weighing about 20 pounds. It is a delicacy for the Inuit, fished traditionally with a spear known as a kakivak. It spawns in fresh water, swimming up Baffin Island's rushing rivers in the spring thaw to glacial lakes, returning to the sea a year later. A freshwater form of this species known as landlocked arctic char (nutillik, in Inuktitut) can be found in some lakes.

Arctic wolf: Grows a shaggy white coat in winter. Unlike the grey and brown wolves elsewhere, which hunt in packs, arctic wolves are usually lone hunters. A male-female pair may hunt together.

Arctic Fox: Another animal that grows a thick white coat as winter approaches, so it blends in with the snow as a disguise while it hunts and to keep it safe from bears and wolves. It has a unique circulation system. Warm blood flows toward the fox's legs and heats up the cool blood returning from its feet. That means that the arctic fox has a warm body and cold feet – ice doesn't stick to its cold pads and toes.

Wolverine: The Inuit used to say that the wolverine is the creator of the world. They look like small bears, just a ball of fur with a long tail. They're in the weasel family and can be just as mean – they have been known to bring down a huge moose. They're smelly, too. Other names for them are 'skunk bear', 'nasty cat' or 'glutton' – not very nice for the creator of the world! One strange fact is that they have a revolving tooth. It's at the back of the mouth and can move 90 degrees or sideways, which allows them to eat frozen food and crush bones. They live isolated lives and almost nothing is known about them, including how many there are in the world.

Arctic Hare: The largest hare in North America. They have small ears to prevent heat loss – but watch out for the black tips to the ears, like an ermine's tail. They eat almost all vegetation, from willow bark to lichen, using their long sharp claws to dig through the snow and long straight incisors (longer and straighter than most hares') to pull plants out of rocky crevices. They can hop on their hind legs like kangaroos, at speeds of up to 30 miles an hour.

Collared Lemming: Related to mice and rats, but bigger and cuter, with white coats in winter. In winter, they also grow long front claws to dig tunnels under the wind-packed snow. There they live, protected from the cold and their enemies.

Snowy Owl: The snowy owl's entire body – even its legs and toes – is covered with soft, fluffy feathers. On top of this coat is yet another coat of overlapping feathers. When temperatures drop, the owl crouches on the ground behind an object that can block the wind. The owl stays still as flying would use up precious heat energy.

Big Beasts

Arctic brown bears: Brown bears, like the tundra grizzly and Kodiaks, live in the Arctic. They dig dens under tree roots and rocks, where they hibernate. Polar bears don't hibernate – though the females do sleep for months on end – and they dig their dens in the snow.

Caribou: Also called reindeer. Both sexes grow antlers. Nobody has ever been able to count the number of caribou on Baffin Island. (There are probably around 180,000 animals.) Most calving takes place on high plateaus. They can run at speeds of 50 miles an hour, travelling great distances, and are good distance swimmers. They are ruminants, with four stomachs – like cows. Their feet adapt according to seasons; in the summer they become soft and spongy to give traction on boggy ground; in the winter, the rim of the hoof is exposed to cut into ice and snow. They mainly eat lichens in winter, especially reindeer moss, pawing through the snow to reach it – an action known as 'cratering'. The rest of the year they will eat anything that grows, from leaves of willows and birches, sedges and grasses. But when starving they will also feed on lemmings, arctic char (fish) and bird eggs. To help them survive extreme cold on exposed plateaus, they have specialised noses with interior bones scrolled like a seashell, or a Cadbury's Flake. As cold air passes over it, it is warmed; and as air leaves the lungs, warmth and dampness is extracted to remain in the body. Like bears they have two kinds of fur to act as insulation.

Walrus: Despite living in freezing water with blocks of ice bobbing around, walruses have a higher body temperature than people. Under an inch-thick hide, there's a six-inch layer of blubber. During the walrus's deep-sea dives to root around for its diet of oysters on the seabed, warm blood shifts away from the skin's surface to inside the body, and its body heat remains stable at about 99°F. When the walrus moves ashore, blood flows back to the skin. It used to be hunted for its ivory tusks – overgrown teeth. A big bull can reach nine or ten feet in length and can weigh over 3,000 pounds.

Really Heavy Stuff

Polar Bears

Quick check list

Its Latin name is Ursus maritimus – which means sea bear.

They are powerful swimmers, with partially webbed feet, and can swim at over 6 miles an hour.

They can swim over 60 miles without rest, but they can drown if tired.

Their nostrils close when diving. They can see underwater.

They have adapted for life on land, sea and ice.

There are only about 30,000 polar bears in the world.

They are officially an endangered species (though licences to hunt are granted to the Inuit).

They live only in Arctic regions – from Alaska to Siberia. Their range is limited only by pack ice.

They have been known to cross the North Pole.

They are carnivores and will eat anything they can kill.

They are the largest land predators. They can weight up to a ton.

A male polar bear is a boar; a female is a sow. A year-old cub is a coy (Cub of the Year).

They can't run too far because they overheat – but can charge like a rhino at 30 m.p.h.

Their fur is translucent – not white. Their skin is black.

Their fur can turn green when it's warm – due to a kind of greenhouse effect, as algae multiplies in the fur.

They rarely drink water.

Female polar bears often don't eat for 8 months.

They give birth in November or December, while in a state like suspended animation (it's not the same as hibernation).

30 million years ago, polar bears shared a common ancestor with the racoon.

A group of polar bears is known as a celebration of bears.

Feast or famine

Polar bears are the world's largest land predators. The average size of a grown male bear is ten feet long standing on all four feet and weighing over half a ton (300-600 kg/660-1,320 lbs); though one shot in Alaska in 1960 was said to weigh some 1001 kg/2,200 lbs – well over a ton. Standing on their hind legs, they can be as a high as an elephant at about eleven and a half feet (3.35m). Female bears are smaller – half the weight and height of a male. Their cubs are very small – barely a pound and a half at birth (600g).

Polar bears are highly specialised killing machines, using tooth and claw. (People have 32 teeth; polar bears have 42 teeth, all like razors.) Their five-inch long claws are like a battery of knives, used to stab, rake and fish seals out of their breathing holes. They are the most carnivorous of the bear family and can smell a seal twenty miles away, smash through yards of ice in minutes to reach their prey and can easily eat about 150 pounds of raw meat in a sitting – that's about 500 Big Macs, a lot of hamburger! In case you think they're greedy, they get by with just one seal a week in the winter and live off their fat in the summer when the ice melts and seals are harder to catch. They are right at the top of the Arctic food chain, with people as their only predators – and sometimes orcas.

Ringed seals are their favourite meal, but they'll also eat anything they can kill (except fish): eider duck eggs, rodents, shellfish, crabs, beluga whales, young walruses, muskox, caribou, reindeer, foxes, wolves, small sea birds – oh, and people. But reindeer and musk oxen can easily outrun a polar bear, and bears overheat quickly, so they subsist almost entirely on live seals and walrus calves, or on the carcasses of dead adult walruses or whales. Adult live walruses are twice the polar bear's weight and hard to handle, while the males' huge 'tusks' (teeth, actually) can inflict great damage to a hungry bear. A really hungry bear will eat berries, roots and kelp in the late summer when there's no ice to catch seals from and pickings are slim. They'll even eat seaweed and rotting flesh – and have been known to raid Inuit hunters' tents and settlements for food. They even eat discarded motor oil – which can kill them. Now motor oil has to be properly disposed of in the Arctic.

Male bears also regularly tuck into the odd snack of a baby polar bear to keep the hunger pangs at bay, which is why mother bears give birth to their cubs as far off the ice edge as possible – where the male bears usually prowl – normally choosing remote, high slopes to dig their dens in the snow under ledges or overhanging rocks where deep snow-drifts have been blown and piled up. Some bears den on sea ice, but thanks to global warming and the early break-up of ice, fewer bears are now doing so.

With all that sea ice, there's not much fresh water – so bears have evolved so that they don't need much. Instead, they get most of the water they need from fat and blubber, which is changed into energy and water in their bodies.

Home sweet home

Polar bear dens are quite like igloos, in that they have a long entrance tunnel (about 6 feet long) which rises up to a cosy chamber, about five feet across and three feet high. Like an igloo, it stays far warmer inside than outside, even in the depths of the coldest Arctic winter's day, rarely dropping below about -2°C. Polar bears have a chemical known as HIT in their blood (hibernation induction trigger) and females – rarely males – will dig a hole and 'hibernate' during the long winter. It's not hibernation, technically speaking, because in hibernation an animal's temperature drops to a very low level whilst in polar bears it remains constant. However, it is similar to hibernation. The whole process of nesting and giving birth is called 'denning'. While the females den, male bears continue to hunt and eat, piling on the weight. At any time of the year, both male and female polar bears will often just dig a hole in the snow during a storm and wait it out.

Not all females fall pregnant; it depends on their body weight. In lean years they don't have enough body fat to go into hibernation for several months, so don't give birth. However, when a female bear is pregnant she dens from November to March or April. Her heart rate drops from seventy beats a minute to eight beats. She doesn't eat, drink, pee or poo – and neither does her temperature drop as with normally hibernating mammals. In this comatose state she gives birth to one or two very small cubs – rarely triplets. Mama Bear's milk is the richest of any bear species – 35% fat; thicker than whipping cream!

Someone passing as spring approaches might be astonished to suddenly see the snow crust break open and a sleek head stick out like a periscope. The head looks in all directions, while the black nose sniffs the air. If it's safe and no marauding male bears are around, the female will pull herself up out of the hole and slowly stretch her stiff muscles and joints. Often she won't stay out for more than a minute or two before disappearing again like a gopher. But soon, she will pop out for longer periods – and eventually, she will ski and roll down the slope, spread-eagled on her back or tummy, all the while working her muscles, getting the tone back in them. Tone and strength is important because as soon as she and her cubs emerge fully and head for the ice to feed, they will be in danger from big male bears. She might need to fight or flee. Sometimes, while she is skiing down the slope, her cub or cubs will suddenly pop up and watch. At first, they are too nervous to leave the den – but when she is ready, she will encourage them to go with her for short trips, until they are steady on their feet.

Finally, when they weigh about 10–12 kg, they head down the slope towards the edge of the sea ice, where Mama Bear will try to find an unwary seal. There is always danger, though, because other bears will be waiting to steal her prey. Her cubs won't go hungry at first because she will continue to provide milk; however, if she doesn't break her fast with a nice plump seal, her milk will dry up and the cubs will starve. Fewer than fifty percent of cubs survive their first year.

Swimming Champ

As well as a relatively small head and long, tapered body to streamline it for swimming, polar bears have partially webbed feet and a thick layer of blubber that adds to their buoyancy and keeps them warm in icy water. Natural oils in their fur mean they don't get waterlogged. Water shakes off and ice doesn't stick to it. They can see under water, and their nostrils close when they dive or forge through waves. But they don't dive after fish or seals. They swim at about 6 miles (10km) an hour. Bears have been spotted by sailors sixty miles from land in the open sea – but it's not really known how far they will swim. However, less sea ice recently means they have to swim further to find their prey and a few bears (four) have been found washed up in the last couple of years – it is believed they drowned after becoming exhausted. Orca whales might catch and eat swimming bears – but contrary to rumour, they don't go after bears on the ice. It is said that polar bears will catch an orca, but this is highly unlikely. Most polar bears weigh about half a ton – and most adult orcas are over five tons. Most likely, bears have been seen eating an already dead whale that has beached.

The invisible bear

Photographers using infrared cameras during the long Arctic night have been astonished to almost stumble into invisible polar bears. They're not ghosts – but it's what happens when infrared filming animals that have transparent coats. Only their breath and black muzzles can be seen through the lens. The polar bear's white fur is not actually white. Each guard hair shaft is pigment-free and transparent with a hollow core. It looks white because the hollow core scatters and reflects visible light, much like ice and snow does, or the water droplets in a cloud. Under the outer, long guard hairs is a thick coat of soft, dense fur to add to the warmth. A polar bear's fur is designed to provide camouflage in the ice and snow to make them almost invisible as they stalk their prey. It's not for protection because until man came along they had no enemies.

It's almost comical to watch a female slip into water and glide through the sea at the edge of an ice shelf, heading for an unwary seal, while her gallumping cub gallops along on the ice, looking at his mother, and almost saying, 'Whatever are you doing? Come up here and watch me play. It's much more fun!' After they've seen a few seals slither off into the safety of deep water, the cub starts to get the message and copies his mum.

Polar bears have black skin under their fur, which absorbs more heat than pale skin. (Their tongues are blue-black like a chow's as well.)

Under that skin is a layer of blubber that is up to 5 inches thick – which is why they can swim in frozen seas and lounge around in temperatures 40°C below freezing without feeling cold. Small neat ears and a short tail help prevent further heat loss.

Bear goggles

You'd have thought that in all that dazzling snow and ice a bear might suffer from snow blindness on a sunny day. But they don't, because their eyes have a protective cover that they can see though, called a nictitating membrane. This cover protects their eyes from the bright sunlight and reflection off the snow and ice. It's a little like having built in goggles. Incidentally, unlike dogs and many other animals, they can see colour. Rather odd, considering it's mostly a whiter shade of pale in the Arctic.

Bear Paws

Polar bears have the largest paws of any animal. They are about a foot across in a grown male, and act as snowshoes. Stiff hairs on their pads and small dimples – like those on a table tennis bat – give them traction so they almost stick to ice and don't sink into snow. People who have observed polar bears covering their black noses with their paws think it is to disguise them so that seals won't spot them – after all, their black noses and muzzles do stand out against the snow. In fact, their noses give out a lot of heat and it's to conserve heat.

Bear brained

The heads of male polar bears are quite small and pointy and narrower than their long necks. Females are the opposite – short necks, big heads. For this reason, the males can't be collared because the collar slips straight off. But females can be fitted with radio collars. This means that only the habits of the females can be studied properly. So while females are safely tucked up in their dens for months on end, their men folk could be up to anything – like hanging out down at the oyster bar shooting pool.

How did they know...?

The word Arctic comes from the ancient Greek Arktikos, or country of the great bear. Historians say that these old Greeks had never seen polar bears, or the Arctic come to that - but they must have done because why else would they have named it after the constellation Ursa Major, the Great Bear, found in the Northern Sky?

Whales

Quick check list
Whales have either teeth or baleen plates to feed.
Baleen is in a whale's upper palette and sieves out microscopic food. It is also known as whalebone – once used in corsets and crinoline skirts.
Blowholes are on the left side of their heads. Some whales have two. They use them to expel stale air when they surface.
Whalesong: whales communicate with sounds that carry for several hundred miles. Some sing, some whistle – or they pop, crackle and hiss like rice crispies.
Most whales use some kind of echolocation or infrasonic sounds to locate prey or to locate their young.
Three different species of whale live permanently in the Arctic: the beluga, the narwhal and the bowhead. Killer whales (orcas), sperm, humpback and blue whales come in the summer.
Their tails are called flukes. They use them to swim and to slap the water.
Logging is when they lie motionless on the surface, tails hanging down.
Lobtailing and tail slaps are when they leap out of the sea or slap the surface, probably for communication, or fun.
Breaching is surging forward fast to (usually) chase their prey onto the shore or ice.
Spyhopping is when they stand on their tails, stick out their heads and rotate like a periscope to check out the hood.

Blue whale: The world's largest living mammals. The largest mammal to ever inhabit the earth, even when gigantic dinosaurs existed. The longest recorded was 106 feet. Heaviest was 150 tons. Endangered, gentle giants, they have been hunted almost to extinction – possibly 1,300–2,000 still exist. They have 300–400 baleen plates and feed on 7,715 pounds of krill and plankton a day (that's about 3.5 tons).

Sperm whale: They break lots of 'biggest' records. They are the biggest toothed whale – each tooth weighs two pounds. They have the biggest brain of any animals (about 20 pounds). Males are about 50–60 feet long and weigh up to 50 tons. Females are a little smaller. They have been known to dive as deeply as 10,500 feet (3,200 m) – average dives are about 4,000 feet (1,200 m). They use echo-location to catch their prey in the dark oceanic depths. The sperm whale can hold its breath for about an hour. When they blow, it goes off like a steam train, 50 feet into the air. Whalers liked sperm whales because of their blubber, which is up to a foot thick. They also vomit up valuable ambergris – which is used in perfume (don't ask). An adult sperm whale can eat about a ton of food each day. The pod bonds for life and mums look after each other's calves.

Bowhead Whale: Huge heads, two blowholes. They don't have teeth, they have baleen plates in the top of their huge mouths, through which they sieve tiny krill and plankton. Females are bigger than males. They are also known as Right Whales (because they were the 'right whales' for old whalers to catch) or Whalebone Whales (for obvious reasons). The largest summer visitor to Baffin Island, they are giants among Arctic whales, reaching almost 40 feet long and weighing 100 tons.

Humpback whale: Baleen feeders, with two blowholes. Their name comes from the way they arch their backs before diving. They're famous for their whalesong – unique, complex and beautiful, sung by the males. Perhaps used for courting, perhaps for talking. The songs are different north and south of the Equator. A song lasts for 10–20 minutes and is repeated for hours. The songs change year by year – almost like a living calendar. They're also very acrobatic. They can throw themselves completely out of the water and swim on their backs with both flippers in the air. They have fun tail lobbing and flipper slapping. They also have a very bizarre way of hunting in pods, called bubble-net feeding. They form a circle about 100 feet across, 50 feet under the surface and blow bubbles as they swim upwards in a spiral path. Their food – krill, plankton or small fish – rises as if in a net of bubbles and they all tuck in to a couple of tons of lovely grub each. They're about 50 feet long and weigh 50 tons.

Orca: Also known as the Killer Whale, orcas hunt in packs like wolves, often chasing their prey right onto a beach or ice shelf. Like most whales, they lobtail, dive, breach, spy hop and tail slap. Females live for about 90 years – twice as long as males. They are known for their distinctive black and white markings. Males can grow to about 30 feet in length and weigh about 6.5 tons. Females are a little smaller.

Beluga whale: They're quite cute – like porpoises, they always seem to be smiling. Because their neck bones aren't fused they can turn their heads, and they love to play with driftwood and foam. Small toothed and ghostly white, they reach about ten to fifteen feet in length and weigh about a ton and a half. They move in pods, wintering in areas of open water or shifting ice, moving northward in the spring. They feed on crustaceans and small fish – using clicks from their nasal passages as echo-locators. They make so many different whistling sounds, they are also known as the sea canary.

Narwhal: They are mottled brown, averaging twelve feet in length, and weigh nearly two tons. But the fascinating thing about them is their horns, which when they surface point straight at the sky. (The Inuit name for them means 'the one that points at the sky'.) When Martin Frobisher's crew found the body of a narwhal on Baffin Island, they stuffed spiders into the tip of the horn. When the spiders all died, they declared it had killed them through magic and so must be a unicorn. (I'm curious as to where they got the spiders from.) Actually, the strange barley-sugar-shaped horn is a tooth, or ivory tusk, that just keeps growing through the upper lip of the male – and they have just two teeth, though one rarely grows. Females sometimes have horns, but they are small and white. But what's the horn for? Recently, a dentist decided that since it was a tooth, someone with experience of teeth should look into it. His surprising discovery unravelled the mystery of the horn. Contrary to all rumours, they don't duel with it, spear ice or hole ships or fish with it. Along its entire length are millions of tiny nerve endings. So the narwhal's mysterious horn is a highly complex sensory organ, that can probably predict the weather – and who knows what else? Perhaps it is magic, after all.

The Science Stuff

CFCs, UV rays and the Ozone hole

One of the books lying around our house is *The Weather Makers* by Tim Flannery, a brilliant Australian scientist and explorer. My dad read it first and one day, when I was idling about, he suggested that I read it. It's a really cool book, stuffed full of the kind of science we should all know about, and written in such a gripping way even non-brainiacs will understand it. Dad had always been interested in environmental issues, but in the last few years, he has grown concerned about the state of the planet and our capacity to self-destruct. When Dad started to look at ways he could help, one of the things he did was to launch the Climate Prize (the Virgin Earth Challenge) to take CO_2 and other harmful gasses out of the atmosphere. He asked Tim to be on the panel. I think it was partly because of this that I really got interested in the environment. When your family is talking about such issues around the dinner table, you can't help getting involved. (And it was my mum who came up with the idea of the Climate Prize in the first place – so it really is a family affair.)

I learned that, as well as CO_2, one of the most destructive things of all are CFCs because they destroy the ozone layer. There was a flurry of concern about CFCs a decade before I was born, when spray cans and refrigeration became demonised for a short time, and then were mostly ignored. But it wasn't until I went on the expedition to Baffin Island that I realised first-hand exactly how important the ozone layer is, what the ozone hole means, and why ultraviolet rays are so destructive to human life.

So what is Ozone and why do we need it?

The oxygen we breathe contains two oxygen atoms joined together (O_2). But high in the stratosphere ultraviolet radiation can force an extra oxygen atom to combine with the duo to make ozone (O_3). Ozone acts as a sunscreen to the world, keeping out ultraviolet light. UV radiation would kill us fast by tearing apart our DNA and our cells.

This is what Tim Flannery has to say about CFCs (I have paraphrased a little):

> The destruction of the ozone layer began long before anyone was aware of it. Fluorocarbons (CFCs and HFCs) had been invented by industrial chemists in 1928, and were found to be very useful for refrigeration, making Styrofoam, as propellants in spraycans, and in air conditioning units. Their remarkable chemical stability (they do not react with other substances) made people confident that there would be few environmental side effects, so they were embraced by industry.
>
> By 1975 spraycans alone were flinging 500,000 tonnes of the stuff into the atmosphere, and by 1985 global use of the main types of CFCs stood at 1,800,000 tonnes. It was their stability, however, that was the key factor in the damage they caused, for they lasted a very long time in the atmosphere.
>
> CFCs evaporate easily, and once released into the great aerial ocean it takes about five years for air currents to waft them into the stratosphere, where UV radiation slowly breaks them

down, causing the release of the chlorine atom. It is the chlorine in CFCs that is so destructive to ozone – just a single atom can destroy 100,000 ozone molecules – and its destructive capacities are maximised at temperatures below –43°C. This is why the ozone hole first emerged over the South Pole, where the stratosphere is a frigid –62°C. At –42°C the stratosphere over the North Pole is balmy by comparison, and it took longer for the chlorine there to deplete ozone to the point that a 'hole' formed.

… It is a matter of dumb luck that our world did not enter a far more severe environmental crisis – perhaps one leading to the collapse of societies – some thirty years ago. This could have occurred if industrial chemists had used bromine instead of chlorine… bromine and chlorine can be used interchangeably for many purposes … and the fact that chlorine was used more often is largely the result of economics, for bromine is somewhat more expensive (and more reactive) than chlorine. Although bromine lasts just one year in the stratosphere, as compared with chlorine's five, bromine is forty-five times more effective in destroying ozone than chlorine.

In areas where the ozone layer has already been depleted, rates of cancer have soared by 60 percent. The Inuit are among the most vulnerable groups. It is not just human bodies that are affected by UV, for the impacts of its increase will be felt throughout the ecosystem. The microscopic single-celled plants that form the base of the ocean's food chain are severely affected by it, as are the larvae of many fish, from anchovy to mackerel. Indeed, anything that spawns in the open is at risk, and a compelling new study shows how that risk is heightened (to 90 per cent

mortality) if accompanied by rising sea temperatures and salinity.

So vulnerable are many marine species that without stratospheric ozone they would go into swift
decline, precipitating a collapse of the ocean's
ecosystems.

This pattern would be repeated on land. The
chilling thing is that had humans found bromine cheaper to use than chlorine we would all
have been enduring unprecedented rates of cancer,
blindness and a thousand other ailments, that our
food supply would have collapsed, and that our
civilisation itself was under intolerable stress.
And we would have had no idea of the cause until
it was too late to react.

Equally chilling is the fact that once the facts were known, industry
squealed in protest and governments refused to act. It was only when
thousands of people kept up the pressure to get CFCs banned that anything happened – and by then damage had been done. Ironically, by
forcing industry to look for alternatives to CFCs they have actually saved
money.

Greenhouse gases

One third of our global emissions of CO_2 gas come from burning fossil
fuels (coal, oil, gas); and two thirds from burning biomass (that's wood,
forests etc.) and nitrogen-containing fertilisers. Two thirds of the energy
from burning fossil fuels is wasted because nineteenth-century technology is used to make our electricity. We burn coal to make steam which
drives turbines, which create energy, which boils a kettle of water. (We
drink 4 billion cups of tea and coffee a day.) For every tonne of fossil
fuel burned in the power stations of the world, 3.5 tonnes of CO_2 gas are
released into the atmosphere.

There are around thirty other greenhouse gases in the atmosphere.
Some are found in trace amounts, but their effect can be far more

proportionately damaging than CO_2. Think of the world under its ceiling – the atmosphere – as a room with a glass ceiling. Each different gas is a pane of glass, letting in light energy, to be trapped in the room as heat.

After CO_2, methane is the next most important gas – and its concentration has doubled in the last hundred years. It's 60 times more potent at capturing heat than CO_2, so if too much is released into the atmosphere, it could be damaging. On the other hand, it doesn't hang around for long. It's made by microbes that thrive in oxygen-less places, like swamps and bowels – so it's in farts and belches, which is why some people bang on the amount of methane cows produce. But there's a lot more than all the cows in the world produce just waiting to be released at the bottom of the sea if we mess about by drilling under the Arctic on the sea bed for minerals and oil, for example. It's also released when frozen tundra thaws – as is happening right now, on a massive scale in both hemispheres and at the top of many high mountain ranges. (See how the school at Clyde River started to collapse, page 37.)

So why are CO_2 and other greenhouse gases so destructive to the environment – and to life?

In a nutshell, they act as a thick, down duvet that traps more heat than we need in our atmosphere. More heat equals melting ice and rising sea levels. New deserts in some places; floods in others. Huge, destructive storms. We should be worried: it could end quite literally in an apocalypse of flood, famine and fire.

Will Steger's Ten Survival Tactics for the Arctic

- Stay hydrated
  It's not easy to make yourself drink water when it's really cold, but staying hydrated is crucial to surviving cold temperatures. When you're well hydrated, you have enough blood volume to keep warm blood pumping to your extremities.

- Consume lots of calories and food high in fat
  Exercising in the cold burns a lot of energy. Global Warming 101 Expedition members need to consume around 5,000 calories per

day including one stick of butter per person per day. Burning these calories produces much-needed body heat.

- Protect yourself from the wind
Wind robs heat from your body as it sneaks into your clothing, replacing warm air with cold. Wind also dries and chills any exposed skin. At -20°F with a 30mph wind, exposed skin will freeze in less than five minutes. A windproof outer layer and a fur ruff around the face are necessities. Inuit people always turn their back to the wind or take shelter behind a komatik sled when possible.

- Insulate yourself from the cold
The thicker the insulation in your clothing and the more air it traps, the warmer you'll be. Any gaps in the insulation, for example between your coat and pants or between your sleeves and gloves, can let a lot of your heat escape. You can also lose a lot of heat by standing, sitting or kneeling on cold surfaces. Thick boots and foam pads can help retain your heat.

- Protect extremities
As your core temperature lowers, your body, in an attempt to maintain its core temperature, restricts blood flow to your extremities. Your body is basically sacrificing your nonessential parts to maintain vital organs. For this reason, hands and feet are often the first parts claimed by frostbite. If you feel your feet or hands getting cold, take aggressive action to rewarm them.

- Stay dry
Your body will lose heat 240 times more quickly to water than to air. If you let your insulation get wet from sweat, snow or water, your insulation will lose much of its ability to keep you warm. Try to adjust your layers *before* you start sweating, and if clothing gets covered in snow, brush off the snow before it melts.

- Don't get lost
Flat light conditions combined with blowing snow and sometimes featureless topography can make navigation difficult. (Flat light is

when the sky is overcast, the horizon blends in with the snow on the ground. No shadows are created, so there is little definition in the texture of the snow which makes it easy to trip when walking around or skiing.) In addition to a GPS and maps, bring enough food and gear with you when you travel on the land. If conditions deteriorate you can dig in and wait for the weather to clear instead of trying to travel in a whiteout.

- Avoid weak ice
  A changing climate, warmer ocean currents and shifting winds can make ice conditions unpredictable. Even traditional travel routes may now be unsafe. Travel with caution. If you do fall through the ice, 'swim' out and roll in the snow to get as much of the water off as possible, then change into dry clothes.

- Practise with all gear before heading out
  In cold temperatures even small tasks like putting on skis, tying a knot or stuffing a sleeping bag take longer and are more difficult. Fumbling with unfamiliar gear or discovering that a crucial item is missing or broken could lead to injury or disaster.

- Take care of each other
  In cold and windy conditions, always check your partners' faces for frostbite and let them know so they can fix it. Try to notice if someone seems cold or low on energy and help them get more food, water and warmth. To be a good safety net for others, however, you must make sure you're taking care of yourself as well.

The Expedition Crew

Will Steger — Team Leader
A formidable voice calling for understanding and the preservation of the Arctic and the Earth, Will Steger is best known for his legendary polar explorations. He has travelled tens of thousands of miles by kayak and dogsled over forty years, leading teams on some of the most significant polar expeditions in history. He lives in the wilderness north of Ely, Minnesota, where he founded

a winter school and developed innovative wilderness programmes. Expedition Leader, team member, educator, polar explorer, photographer, writer and lecturer, Steger has become a voice calling for understanding and the preservation of the Arctic. He is the author of four books: Over the Top of the World, Crossing Antarctica, North to the Pole and Saving the Earth. Read Will Steger's past expedition journals at www.willsteger.com.

John Stetson – Expedition Manager

Stetson has travelled over 80,000 miles by dog team over the last 20 years, primarily in the Arctic and sub-Arctic regions. Since 1986, he has been highly involved with sled dogs as an educator, explorer/ adventurer and as a professional racer. He has been a leader of several world-class expeditions, a team member on numerous others, in addition to being a consultant and dog trainer for many expeditions. Stetson is a highly regarded and gifted sled dog trainer. Stetson's love of the Arctic and its inhabitants led him to found Hudson Bay Adventures in 1995. Located in Churchill, Manitoba, on the coast of Hudson Bay, Hudson Bay Adventures has educated thousands of people on the use of sled dogs and their historical place in the Arctic. Stetson is married to his partner and the love of his life Shelly Stetson and they have a wonderful son – Nelson, aged five. (Nelson joined us on the very last leg of the expedition.)

Abby Fenton – Education Co-ordinator and Expedition Member

Fenton, a native of Boston, Massachusetts, developed a love of wilderness early in life. She spent her first night in a tent with her parents at the age of two. As a child she grew up camping and canoeing with her family in Maine. She has spent five years working for the Voyageur Outward Bound School leading backpacking, climbing and dogsledding expeditions for all ages in northern Minnesota and the Rocky Mountains of Montana. She is passionate about connecting kids of all ages with the outdoors and the environment through experiential education.

Elizabeth Andre – Education Co-ordinator and Expedition Member

Andre spent ninety-six weeks of her first sixteen years of life at sleep-away summer camp. Her love of outdoor exploration that germinated at summer camp grew as a college student at the Iowa

Lakeside Laboratory, where she participated in an archaeological dig, collected plant specimens from quaking bogs and mapped glacial-stagnation topography using surveying equipment. Then, as a student at the Wild Rockies Field Institute, an expedition-based college-level academic field school, it blossomed into her passion: environmental education through expeditions. Her doctoral work in education, as well as her experience leading dogsled expeditions for Outward Bound Schools, connected her with Will Steger and the 2007 expedition to Baffin Island.

Nancy Moundalexis – Dog Trainer and Expedition Member
Nancy hails from King George, Virginia. Her love for nature and adventure grew out of her time at a science-based Nature Camp where she was a camper and counsellor. She has instructed canoeing and dogsledding for Outward Bound courses over a period of four years. Now Nancy spends her summers working in the Boundary Waters Canoe Area Wilderness for the Forest Service and runs sled dogs in the winter.

Inuit Expedition Team Members

Theo Ikummaq – Expedition Member and Inuit Partner
Theo Ikummaq is an Inuit hunter and explorer who has experienced the effects of global warming first-hand. He is a trained expert on moving ice and travel in the Arctic region of Baffin Island. Theo was born in an igloo on 20 January 1955 in the town of Iglulik, Nunavut. He spent his teenage years at an outpost camp on Baffin Island, using only a short-wave radio for communications. From 1979 to 1982, he studied Renewable Resources Technology Management at Fort Smith College in the Northwest Territories, Canada. His skills include hunting techniques, wildlife and animal behaviour observation, arctic survival, and shelter building. Theo has lived in and explored remote areas of Greenland, Arctic Bay, Iqaluit, Broughton Island and Ottawa, Canada. In 1987, he travelled on the Ultima-Thule Expedition by dogsled from Iglulik, Nunavut, to Thule, Greenland. The expedition travelled 3,100km and included five team members with three teams of dogs, building igloos along the way for shelter. Theo has worked with National Geographic on Four Cultures – Life on Baffin Island and Isuma Productions on Journals of Knut Rasmussen and The Fast Runner.

He is the co-author of the book Ice Thru Inuit Eyes. He currently lives with his wife, Lydia, in Iglulik, Nunavut.

Lukie Airut — Inuit hunter
Lukie was born in 1942 and spent his young years at an outpost camp outside of Iglulik. He is a hunter and has held a variety of different jobs over the years. Lukie is a celebrated carver and has been a member of the Canadian Rangers for fifteen years. He has spent more than thirty years running dogs and brings a lot of knowledge of Inuit traditional ways to the expedition team. Lukie lives in Iglulik with his wife Marie and has nine children.

Simon Qamanirq — Inuit hunter
Born in 1953, Simon spent most of his life in Arctic Bay in northern Baffin Island. He remained there until he moved to Iglulik last year with his wife Eunice and six-year-old son Ishmael. He makes his livelihood as a hunter and carver. Simon is a renowned artisan and has travelled widely in Europe and Alaska to demonstrate and exhibit his carving. He is a member of the Canadian Rangers and a Northwest Territory Craft Council Member. He is also a polar bear hunting guide and skilled dog driver.

Expedition Base Camp Members

John Huston — Expedition Base Camp Manager
John is a wilderness and Arctic expeditioner, experiential educator, writer, world traveller, cross-country ski racer and fledgling historian. In the spring of 2005, John completed a 1,400-mile ski and dogsled expedition on the Greenland Ice Cap with a team of four Norwegians. During the spring and summer of 2006, he worked as expedition manager for the One World Expedition, the first expedition to reach the North Pole in the summer. As Global Warming 101 Expedition Base Camp Manager, John handles all of the expedition logistics and communications with the team in the field. John is planning to ski unsupported to the North Pole in 2009. Visit www.forwardexpeditions.com for more information on this expedition.

Jim Paulson — Webmaster and Expedition Technology Logistics
Jim is an integral member of the expedition base camp crew, and knows everything about technology. Through the use of modern

genetic testing it has been determined that Jim was born from Viking stock. As an infant he was found floating in the Arctic Ocean by a wide-ranging, roving mother mountain lion. Even as an infant Jim had a full beard and full head of hair. This somewhat confused Mama Mountain Lion, but she adopted him and raised him in a cave with her small litter of cubs as any good mother would.

Jerry Stenger – Expedition Cameraman and Producer
Jerry Stenger was raised in Mankato, Minnesota and developed an early appreciation for camping and nature. He attended the University of St Thomas in St Paul and received his undergraduate degree in television production. First joining Will in 1989 when he was preparing for his International Trans-Antarctica Expedition, Jerry continues to produce, shoot and edit video programming for Steger's projects.

Guest Expedition Members

Ed Viesturs
Washington resident Ed Viesturs is widely regarded as America's foremost high-altitude mountaineer. He is familiar to many from the 1996 IMAX Everest Expedition documentary. In the autumn of 2006 Viesturs released his autobiography, No Shortcuts To The Top. He has successfully reached the summits of the world's fourteen 8,000m peaks without supplemental oxygen. Viesturs has been one of the most successful Himalayan climbers in American history. Check out www.edviesturs.com.

Sarah McNair-Landry
No stranger to cold weather, Sarah grew up in Iqaluit from the age of three. Shortly after turning seventeen she went on her first extended expedition, crossing the Greenland Ice Cap with her parents and older brother Eric. A year later she travelled to the South Pole on a 71-day kite-ski expedition with her mother and brother. Recently Sarah travelled to the North Pole on a 100-day dogsled expedition with her father and two British explorers. Sarah and her 22-year-old brother Eric are returning to Greenland to cross the ice cap vertically by kite-ski, travelling 1,429 miles/2,300km over the course of two months. The goal of the expedition is to inspire youth around the globe to reach their dreams. See – www.pittarak.com.

Index